Thomas Baldwin Thayer

Over the River

Or, Pleasant walks into the valley of shadows, and beyond. A book of consolations

for the sick, the dying, and the bereaved

Thomas Baldwin Thayer

Over the River
Or, Pleasant walks into the valley of shadows, and beyond. A book of consolations for the sick, the dying, and the bereaved

ISBN/EAN: 9783337233570

Printed in Europe, USA, Canada, Australia, Japan

Cover: Foto ©Andreas Hilbeck / pixelio.de

More available books at **www.hansebooks.com**

OVER THE RIVER;

OR,

Pleasant Walks into the Valley of Shadows,

AND BEYOND:

A BOOK OF CONSOLATIONS FOR THE SICK, THE DYING, AND THE BEREAVED.

BY THOMAS BALDWIN THAYER.

BOSTON:
UNIVERSALIST PUBLISHING HOUSE,
No. 37 CORNHILL.
1871.

Entered according to Act of Congress, in the year **1864**, by

TOMPKINS & COMPANY,

In the Clerk's Office of the District Court of the District of Massachusetts.

TO

THE MEMORY OF

ABEL TOMPKINS,

AT WHOSE REQUEST IT WAS UNDERTAKEN,

THIS VOLUME

IS AFFECTIONATELY INSCRIBED.

PREFACE.

BESIDE those named in the title-page, this little volume has two objects specially in view—

First: To present the subject of death in its true light; to show that the Scriptures speak of it cheerfully, and in pleasant phrase; to establish the fact that, as a rule, it is not attended either with the mental terror, or the extreme physical suffering, commonly ascribed to it—and thus to remove that dread of dying which oppresses the minds and hearts of so many truly good persons, and is the cause of no little unhappiness to all who are passing down to the banks of the river of death.

Second: To offer for the consideration of the thoughtful believer, more elevated and satisfactory views of the future state than prevail generally among Christians. When we consider the extent, the grandeur and variety of the material universe, the countless worlds which throng the abysses of space; it is surely reasonable to suppose that, since we cannot, while in the body, behold the wonders of God's creative power as displayed in these, we shall be permitted to visit them out of the body. It is difficult to believe that with all these glories of God's creation calling to us from afar, we shall remain in any one place, singing hymns and playing on golden harps through eternal ages, and think this heaven — whatever the meaning we attach to these expressions.

The book is sent forth as a Comforter, in these times when so many need comfort and courage and faith, with a prayer that the blessing of God may attend it on its mission of mercy.

Boston, May, 1864.

CONTENTS.

I.

Comfort for the Sick.

THE REVELATIONS OF SICKNESS,..................... 11
REASONS FOR THANKFULNESS,.......................... 26
GOOD IN EVIL,.. 34
THE BLESSING OF A CHEERFUL PIETY,................ 42
IS THY HOUSE IN ORDER?........................... 54
INSPIRED MEDITATIONS FOR THE SICK CHAMBER,...... 61
DIVINE CONSOLATIONS FOR THE SICK,................ 66

II.

Revelations for the Dying.

"OVER THE RIVER,"................................... 75
THE EARTHLY TENT — THE HEAVENLY HOUSE,.......... 85
FALLING ASLEEP,.................................... 98
THE DEATH OF THE BODY THE LIFE OF THE SPIRIT,..107

THE PASSAGE OF THE RIVER AND THE PREPARATION
    FOR IT,..119
THE WORLD BEYOND THE RIVER, OR THE GLORY OF
    THE CELESTIAL,..................................129
EMPLOYMENTS OF THE FUTURE LIFE,....................137
THE ATTRACTIONS OF HEAVEN,.........................150
ATTRACTIONS OF EARTH,..............................159
THE DYING DO NOT SUFFER,...........................171

III.

Consolations for the Bereaved.

THE LESSONS OF SORROW,.............................187
THE SOUL'S HUNGER AND THE BREAD OF HEAVEN,.........193
THROUGH TRIBULATION INTO THE KINGDOM,..............200
PEACE IN BELIEVING,................................210
DEATH OF HUSBAND OR WIFE,..........................217
COMFORT THE CHILDREN,..............................228
THE DEATH OF CHILDREN,.............................235
THE MEMORY OF THE DEAD,............................248
THE DEAD NEVER GROW OLD,...........................256
"THE VALLEY OF PEACE," OR THE PLACE OF THE
    DEAD,..263

Comfort for the Sick.

The Lord will strengthen him upon the bed of languishing: thou wilt make all his bed in sickness.—Psalm xli. 3.

Chamber of sickness! much to thee I owe,
    Though dark thou be;
The lessons it imports me most to know,
    I owe to thee!
A sacred seminary thou hast been,
I trust, to train me for a happier scene.

Chamber of sickness! suffering and alone,
    The world withdrawn,
The blessed beams of heavenly truth have shone
    On me, forlorn,
With such a hallowed vividness and power,
As ne'er were granted to a brighter hour.

I.

The Revelations of Sickness.

> In silence will I bear the pain
> Which God has sent me by his will;
> Ne'er will I murmur nor complain;
> Although he wounds, he loves me still.
> In sickness not the less God's child
> Than if the world around me smiled.
> True to himself, God changes never—
> Wise, mighty, merciful, forever.

THE lesson of suffering is, of all others, the most reluctantly learned; and yet it has often proved the most instructive and beneficial of all, bringing with it blessings which abide with us through life and death, and reach over even into the immortal sphere—"for our light affliction, which is but for a moment, worketh for us a far more exceeding and eternal weight of glory." Sickness, sorrow, bereavement, death, are but the servants of God, teaching us heavenly things, revealing to us the mystery of Divine Love forever educing good from evil; and finally leading us up into the heavenly heights, whose clearer atmosphere enables us to see things in their true relations, and to discern afar off the beneficent results of our present trials.

And yet, believing this, we do not love sorrow, we do not choose suffering, because of any good it may secure us. This is not surprising, when we consider the weakness and blindness of human nature. The boy who does not wish to go to school, still wishes for the knowledge which is the fruit of diligent study. So we do not like to suffer; but we rejoice in the new life and heavenly-mindedness which often are the product of it. We thank God for the gift of immortal life; yet we do not like death, which is the only gate that leads to it. We believe in the ineffable joys of heaven, but we still cling to the comparatively poor and transient joys of earth.

This is well, for if there were no natural dread of death, no instinctive shrinking from its touch, we should desert the post of duty, and rashly fling life away on the first occasion of grief or misfortune. As it is, the matter is so disposed by the Lord of life and death, that, as a rule, however difficult our duties, however great our sorrows, we are willing to stay; while, at the same time, he has given us such blessed hopes and consolations that, rightly accepted, we are willing to go when he calls us.

And so, my suffering friend, it is not a matter of wonder, that you cannot welcome sickness and bodily pain, or that you find them hard to bear, even though you may believe they are not wholly evil. But that the burthen may be lightened, let us commune together for a little of the things which the Lord hath spoken for your comfort and encouragement; and of the benefits coming from affliction accepted in an humble and teachable spirit. And,

First: Sickness reveals to every one the need of religious culture, and the value of religious faith; and one of its obvious benefits is that it affords opportunity for reflection and meditation on this important theme. It may be that you have not hitherto given much thought to religious things, to the Bible, to God, to the nature and needs of your own soul. The world, its cares, and gains, and ambitions, have wholly engrossed your attention; and spiritual things have been pushed aside, forgotten or driven out of mind in the hurry and eager rush of your worldly life. Possibly it has never seriously occurred to you that sickness and suffering and death might fall to your lot; that this life is brief at the longest; and that, by and by, you must pass on "over the river," and leave behind you all you have, and all you love.

But now you will have time to think of these things; and you will discover that you are not quite sufficient for yourself; that health and strength may suddenly depart, and the frail thread of life be snapped at any moment, and that it is wise to be prepared for it. Prostrated upon the bed of sickness, withdrawn from the excitements and interests which have so long held you in bondage, a favorable and fitting season is granted you for self-communion and reflection on these grave and paramount questions. And, brought face to face with the great realities, you will begin to prepare for the new experience born of them, in an earnest and humble spirit, — and then the blessing is not afar off.

Second: This sickness will reveal to you your entire and constant dependence on God; and how it is that you live, and move, and have all your blessings, in him. Through all these years God has been your support and protection, the source of life and health, and the giver of every good and perfect gift you have enjoyed. But how often have you remembered him with gratitude and thanksgiving for these blessings? How often have you sought the guidance of his wisdom, the blessing of his holy spirit? How often have you prayed for strength to overcome the temptations and to bear the trials which might meet you in the difficult paths of life? But now you will think of God. Weak and feeble, and suffering under the hand of disease, you will turn to him for comfort and strength; and you will find him a very present help in time of trouble, for the ear of the Lord is ever open to them that call upon him.

And what a blessed thing it is, even at the cost of sickness and bodily anguish, to be able to shake off the entanglements of the world; and worn, weary and fainting, to lie, as it were, on the bosom of the Father, to feel his supporting arm underneath you, and to hear his voice speaking to you in the silence and saying: "Fear not; when thou passest through the waters I will be with thee; and through the rivers, they shall not overflow thee; when thou walkest through the fire, thou shalt not be burned, neither shall the flame kindle upon thee; for I have redeemed thee, I have called thee by thy name; thou art mine." This is the promise of the Lord to all who seek him in the time of need. He is a sure refuge and defence in all our troubles; our strength, our peace and joy, our health, our life, our all. And that sickness is a blessing which leads the sufferer to the experimental test of this truth, and reveals to him that his highest life, his supreme good, is in God, and lies infinitely above the health or sickness, the life or death, of the body.

Lean, then, upon the strong arm of the Father, and let your soul open out toward him in holy communion, as the fainting flower opens to receive the welcome and refreshing rain. Let this affliction draw you unto him through Christ, and you will find all and more than you seek. In the quiet of your chamber, in the secret sanctuary of the spirit, lift up the prayer of faith and trust; and you will feel ere long that the peace of God is finding its way into your heart, and the grace of our Lord Jesus Christ making the burthen lighter and easier to bear every day.

O there is no experience of the soul so sweet and comforting, so divinely beautiful, as that which brings us, through sorrow and suffering, into this close relation with our Heavenly Father; and by which we are able to recognize the touch and pressure of his arm as it passes under us to hold us up in our weakness. To lie down upon it, and cease from all effort and struggle; to feel that it is not your own, but God's strength that sustains you; to feel a sweet calm diffused through all your being, that perfect peace passing knowledge or expression; to be patient and strong under suffering, and know all the time that you never could feel thus by your own unaided effort; that it is all of the Lord's mercy and goodness, that he helps you, holds you in his arms, and does every thing for you; and that therefore all weariness is gone, and all the anguish of suffering, and the bitterness of death, and nothing now can disturb you evermore. O, when this heavenly height is reached, however rough and dark the path that leads to it, we are thankful to have trodden it. This divine calm which possesses the soul, is more than an equivalent for all that we have suffered. And we feel that out of our hearts we can truly bless God for that sickness and pain which have thus brought us into the fellowship of his Spirit; for that sorrow which has brightened now into everlasting peace.

Third: This sorrow will reveal to you the greatness and tenderness of the Saviour's love, and bring you into closer sympathy with him; for he was "a man of sorrows and acquainted with grief," and is therefore "touched with the feeling of our infirmities," and "in that he himself hath suffered" he is able and ready to succor them that come to him. Hence he says, "Come unto me all ye that labor and are heavy-laden, and I will give you rest: take my yoke upon you, and learn of me; for my yoke is easy, and my burden is light, and ye shall find rest unto your souls." There is something affecting in the thought that Jesus has trodden all the paths of suffering humanity, tasted every cup of bitterness, and at last met death in its most fearful form — all for us; that he might know how to pity us in our grief and anguish, and to comfort us in our distresses, and how to strengthen and encourage us in the day of death, and give us victory over the grave. O, how much nearer and dearer he seems to us on this account; how much greater our confidence and affection, and how are we comforted and strengthened in all our afflictions, when we think of this sublime sacrifice for our good!

Let this season of affliction, then, direct your thoughts to the meek and gentle One, the Divine Sufferer, "who was made a little lower than the angels for the suffering of death, and crowned with glory and honor, that he by the grace of God should taste death for every man." Think of him as the

Comforter and the example of all who suffer; and remember with what sweetness and patience he bore his burthens, saying, meekly, "the cup which my Father giveth me shall I not drink it?" And remember, too, that he is **still near to** all who will call upon **him; that** now, as of old, he **is** "passing **by," and** is ready to heal and to bless every **suffering** soul.

>Watcher, who wakest by the bed of pain,
>While the stars sweep on in their midnight train,
>Stifling the tear for thy loved one's sake,
>Holding thy breath lest his sleep should break,
>In thy lowliest hour there's a helper nigh —
>>Jesus of Nazareth passeth **by**.

>Fading one, with the hectic streak,
>And the veins of fire, on thy wasted cheek,
>Fearest thou the shade of the darkened vale,
>Look to the Guide who can never fail;
>He hath trod it himself; he will hear thy sigh —
>>Jesus of Nazareth passeth by.

>Mourner who sittest in the churchyard lone
>Scanning the lines on that marble stone,
>Plucking the weeds from the grassy bed,
>Planting the rose and the myrtle instead,
>Look up from the tomb with a tearless eye —
>>Jesus of Nazareth passeth by.

Fourth: Sickness reveals the value of the Bible as a source of comfort and encouragement. There is a beautiful significance in the words of Walter Scott, when approaching death, respecting the preciousness of the Divine Scripture to the sick and dying. He had requested his son-in-law to read to him; and, on his inquiring what book he should read from, the sufferer exclaimed, as he looked up, his face illuminated with a heavenly expression, "What book! why, my dear, to one in my situation, there *is* but one book!" There is pointed truth in this. In the hour of our greatest need, when disease and pain are doing their sad work on the burning brain and the throbbing heart, when the spirit and the flesh fail, and there is no help in man — it is not the revelations of science that we wait for, but the Revelations of the Gospel. It is not what the geologist may say of earth, but what the Spirit says of heaven; not the words of Plato nor of Bacon, but the words of Jesus and Paul, that the fainting heart welcomes as the balm of healing, as the sweetest and the only comfort it knows. In that hour, in that condition, truly there *is* but one book for us. All others are valuable only as they serve to illustrate the spirit and teachings of that, and help us to appropriate to our own needs its divine promises and consolations.

And how rich the Bible is in these words of eternal life and peace. And now that you are weary and distressed, this will be made manifest unto you, and the sacred volume will become a lamp to your feet and a light to your path, so long as you are in the valley of shadows. It will be to you as a new book, every page seemingly illuminated with truth especially spoken for you; every testimony of the Father's love, every promise of comfort and divine assistance, coming with a fresh meaning, and a wonderful adaptedness to your particular condition of mind and heart. And whatever may be the result of this sickness, whether you stay with us, or go to join the departed over the river, it will bestow one abiding blessing, if it lead you thus to the Fountain of Life, the wells of living water. And in that day thou shalt say, "O Lord, I will praise thee: though thou hast afflicted me, yet thy chastisement is turned away, and thou hast comforted me. Behold, God is my salvation; I will trust, and not be afraid: for the Lord Jehovah is my strength and my song; he also is become my salvation. Therefore with joy will I draw water out of the wells of salvation."

Go then, thou sick and weary and failing one, go to the word of God for strength and resignation. Turn over the glowing pages of the gospels, linger among its inspired utterances, treasure up in your heart the sweet sayings of Jesus; and you will find the sick bed eased, the hours of pain shortened, the power of endurance daily increasing, and a calm courage and a holy peace possessing your soul.

Of health and strength and ease bereft
   My spirit turns to Thee —
O hast thou not a blessing left,
   A blessing, Lord, for me?
Behold thy prisoner — loose my bonds,
   If 'tis thy gracious will,
If not, O make me, Lord, content
   To be thy prisoner still!
I may not to thy house repair,
   Yet here thou surely art;
Lord, consecrate a house of prayer
   In my surrendered heart.

To faith reveal the things unseen;
   To hope the joys unfold;
Let love, without a veil between,
   Thy glory now behold.
Oh! make thy face on me to shine,
   That doubt and fear may cease;
Lift up thy countenance benign
   On me, and give me peace.

II.

Reasons for Thankfulness.

If what I wish thy will denies,
It is that thou art good and wise ;
Afflictions which may make me mourn,
Thou canst, thou dost, to blessings turn.

Deep, Lord, upon my thankful breast,
Let all thy favors be imprest ;
And though withdrawn thy gifts should be,
In all things I'll give thanks to thee.

SICK, languishing and despondent, I lie here through the long day, and through the longer night, counting the weary hours as they drag heavily by. Deprived of ease and comfort, struggling with bodily pains, with the burning heat of the fever, with the protracted and exhausting cough of consumption, with faintness and feebleness — it is hard to bear it all with patience and resignation. It is hard to give up health and business, all the duties and pleasures and welcome activities of life, and lie down upon the bed of sickness and suffering, and perhaps of death.

Yes, but after all, have I not many things to be thankful for? With all that I suffer, have I not much to comfort me? With all the blessings taken, are there not many more than these left to me? What cause for gratitude, since I am sick, that I am sick at home, among my own kindred, surrounded with the familiar things and the familiar faces which have made such happiness for me all my life long. O what a difference, if this sickness had come upon me in a foreign land, or far away from home, among strangers, with no friends or relatives to minister to my wants, or speak sweet words of consolation and hope.

Thanks to the merciful providence of God, since this affliction has come, it has come under circumstances so favorable, and so well calculated to lighten the burthen of it. What a comfort it is to see the dear faces of those I love, to hear their pleasant voices, to recognise their light step upon the floor, to know that the pain-assuaging draught is mixed, and held to my lips, by the hand of affection. How it helps me to bear my pain, this thoughtful kindness, this constant ministration of patient, never-tiring love! How it redeems the weariness of the day, and peoples the loneliness of the night, and lights up the gloom of the sick chamber. And if I die, O how blessed it is to die among mine own; to know that, as my eyes grow dim, their last look will be of those ever dear to me; and that the last sounds which will linger in my failing ears, will be the sweet voices of the beloved who have given to my life all its beauty and joy. O God, my heavenly Father, I thank thee for these mercies; and though in thy wisdom thou hast afflicted me, and taken back some of thy gifts, I will not forget the many precious blessings left. "Because thy loving kindness is better than life, my lips shall praise thee."

There is another cause for thankfulness, blending in with that first named, which also reveals to me the fact, that this sickness is not wholly evil. Hitherto, absorbed in my own affairs, anxious for my own interest, and blessed with health, I have thought too little of others, — the sick and suffering and dying. I have seldom visited the house of sorrow and mourning, seldom spoken a word of sympathy to those in affliction. And I have not been prompt to offer my services in such cases, and to give heed to the many little duties and attentions, which are so grateful to the sick, and serve so much to lighten the gloom, and lift up the weight of suffering.

I am thankful that my affliction has taught me the worth of these things, and shown me what comfort there is to the sick in words of kindly remembrance and inquiry, in the timely visit, in the delicate attentions of friends, in the generous fellowship of a loving spirit; in a word, in the sweet consciousness that all around there are hearts beating in every pulse with sympathy, with earnest wishes and prayers for our welfare. I know now what inspirations of hope and courage and cheerfulness there are in these things. This baptism of affliction has quickened my soul into new and tender relations to all who suffer. Hereafter the sick man is twice my brother — by the ties of a common humanity, and by the fellowship of a common sorrow. Hereafter my feet shall be swift to do the offices of love, and to repay to others sick the debt of kindness laid on me. The word of cheer, the friendly visit, the timely remembrance, shall not be wanting from me to make the weary hours of the sick chamber pass quickly, to lay the heavy pains to rest, to quiet the agitated nerves, and close the long sleepless eyes in soothing slumbers.

Surely it is something to be thankful for, even if it come through sickness; this knowledge of myself; this quickened sense of my dependence on the kindness and sympathy of friends, and the consequent duty I owe to others; this sweet experience of the comfort there is in human sympathy in the day of distress; and the divine joy there is in ministering to the afflicted, in following Christ in his work of mercy among the sick and suffering.

And then, what reason have I to be thankful, that in the providence of God, the lines of life have fallen to me in a land of Christian knowledge and faith; that through all this weary sickness I have the comforting promise of the Gospel, that whatever of suffering is laid upon me will in some way turn to my good. What should I do in this day of darkness and distress, if I felt that all my trials and sorrows, that all events indeed, came of chance, without order or law, without any beneficial purpose or end! But now, thanks to the merciful and loving Jesus, I am consoled by the confident assurance I have, that all things are subject to the divine rule; that there is no chance nor accident in my afflictions, but that all, past, present and to come, is directed by infinite benevolence, and that therefore every pain and grief of mine will finally shape itself into some form of blessing.

O, then, cannot I bear patiently, sustained by this inspiring truth? And, however dark the night, shall I not walk forward cheerfully, with this promise of the Lord as a shining light in my soul, illuminating all the path before me?

Yes, in my sickness I will thankfully remember the blessings of home and kindred; I will be devoutly grateful for the ministrations of love and friendship; and, whatever my sufferings, I will rejoice in the comforting promises of the Father, that all shall end well.

> All as God wills, who wisely heeds
>   To give or to withhold,
> And knoweth more of all my needs
>   Than all my prayers have told!
> Enough that blessings undeserved
>   Have marked my erring track;
> That wheresoe'er my feet have swerved,
>   His chastening turned me back. —

That more and more a Providence
  Of love is understood,
Making the springs of time and sense
  Sweet with eternal good;
That care and trial seem at last
  Through Memory's sunset air,
Like mountain ranges overpast
  In purple distance fair, —

That death seems but a covered way
  Which opens into light,
Wherein no blinded child can stray
  Beyond the Father's sight, —
And so the shadows fall apart,
  And so the west winds play;
And all the windows of my heart
  I open to the day.

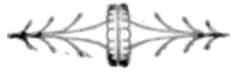

III.

Good in Evil.

>   One adequate support
> For the calamities of mortal life
> Exists, one only, — an assured belief
> That the procession of our fate, howe'er
> Disturbed or sad, is ordered by a Being
> Of infinite benevolence and power,
> Whose everlasting purposes embrace
> All accidents, converting them to good.

NO evil is wholly evil! This is one of the bright gleams of light that stream in upon all nights, even the darkest. No evil is wholly evil. Behind the blackest cloud the sun shines — or the stars. All our trials and sorrows have elements of good in them; hopeful features which smile upon us in gentle reproof of our unbelief and discouragement. Now and then, as the swift shuttle passes, we catch glimpses of bright threads weaving themselves into the dark web of our affliction. Hidden relations of events are discovered in this or that direction, where we did not look for them. And, by and by, the future good, which at first was shut out by the present and nearer evil, begins to lift itself into the line of vision; and we feel our faith increased, and confirmed at last, in the ever joint action of the infinite Power and Love of the father.

Long time ago I wrote thus; and, as the years drift by, and the sphere of observation and experience is extended, and I discover how singularly the threads of good and evil, joy and sorrow, sickness and health, cross and recross as warp and woof in the loom of life, and intertwine and weave up into the web of destiny; the more firmly do I believe this, the greater is my confidence in that wisdom, which ordains evil as well as good, which orders with equal mercy darkness and light, suffering and rejoicing, death and life. Day by day, and year by year, the divine fact comes into clearer light, that all evil has a sunny side to it, that sorrow is the twin-sister of joy, and the grave only the vestibule to the temple of immortal life.

> "There is no sorrow, friends, but it has still
> Some soul of sweetness in it; there's no ill
> But comes from Him who made it, and is good
> As fruit in season, leaf in budding wood."

This affliction that has come upon you, this sickness that consumes your strength, and wastes the body, and withdraws you from the activities of life, is not in vain, not without some purpose of good for you. Receive it in a trusting spirit; improve it in lifting up the soul to God. Let the weary hours of weakness and pain be lightened by thoughts of heavenly things, by sweet communion with the Holy Spirit; by recollections of past events, which have revealed the good there is always hidden away in evil, which have shown the benefit there is in every grief or trial that the Lord appoints; by numbering to yourself the occasions in your own life, and in the life of others, when you have seen how much better it was that God's will was done rather than yours or theirs.

A thousand times have I repeated to myself these lines, whose truth is equal to their beauty:

> "With patient heart thy course of duty run,
> God nothing does, nor suffers to be done,
> But thou wouldst do thyself, if thou couldst only see
> The *end* of all he does, as well as he."

Nothing seems to me more certain than this. With all my soul I believe that if we could see the end of all we suffer as clearly as God sees it, we should not lift a finger to change it. However deeply the iron might enter the soul, however bitter the cup of our afflictions, how great soever the wreck of our hopes and plans on the sea of adversity, — still, if we could understand the purposes of God, the exact thing he means to accomplish by our trials, the thing he is doing we should do ourselves.

In the depth of his distress Jacob exclaims: "Me have ye bereaved, Joseph is not, and Simeon is not, and now ye will take Benjamin away — all these things are against me." Poor old man! These things *seem* to be against you, but they are not. They are all *for* you; they are the very things you would do yourself, if you only knew the significance of them. They are not evil, but good; not death, but life to you and yours. What a lesson of humility and faith this story teaches: Joseph pleading in anguish of soul with his brethren, that they will not make him governor of Egypt, and the savior of his family and kindred! Jacob bitterly weeping over an affliction, which was only the angel of God waiting to restore to him his long lost son! How ought these to rebuke our murmuring and impatience, when sickness, or bereavement, or any kind of misfortune falls to our lot.

So *we* misjudge the ways of God, and miscall his providences. The names we give to the divine methods and agencies make sad confusion of the truth. We call this good and that evil to-day; but to-morrow reveals our mistake, corrects our judgment, and compels a change in our vocabulary.

The boy of ten, who sees happiness only in kites and balls, in sleds and skates, thinks it a sore affliction to be shut up in the hated school-house, under a stern master, compelled to learn the hardest lessons — this to him is the greatest evil you can put upon him. But, as the years flow on, and bear him forward into the activities of life, he finds that the greatest evil at ten, has changed into the greatest good at thirty, and opened for him ways of wealth and usefulness, and set him in the high places of honor and power.

I think it is so with all our trials — yea, with all the evils of our world — that there is a germ of good in them, which by and by buds and blossoms into fruit. We do not like much the black and smutty charcoal, but it is what nature makes her diamonds of. The evil we suffer is only the black and sooty carbon, which, when the necessary conditions are present, is converted into good, into the brilliant and valuable diamond. We ought, therefore, to be very slow in our judgment of the ways of Providence.

What we need most of all, what you need, my suffering friend, is, *Trust in God.* Try to learn this lesson, and to apply it now in the days of your tribulation, when the body sinks under disease, and the spirit faints; when your hopes grow dim, and the clouds begin to drift between you and the setting sun, and a darkness as of the night gathers about you. How beautiful was the simple faith of our childhood, when, however dark the night, however devious the way, we were ready to put our hand into the hand of father or mother, and walk forward with unfaltering heart, confident they would lead us to the shelter and security of our dear home.

Accept and cherish the same sweet and childlike faith in God, who is also our

Father. The path, by which he brings you on your way, may sometimes lead out into the darkness and the desert, may, as in the case of Joseph, lead down into Egypt; but forget not that God dwells in the prisons and palaces of Egypt, as well as in the tents of Jacob; that he is present everywhere, and always, as a Refuge and a Comforter. Be patient and hopeful, therefore; remembering that, however this sickness may terminate, the hour approaches, —

> "When all the vanities of Life's brief day
> Oblivion's hurrying hand shall sweep away;
> And all its sorrows, at the wakening blast
> Of the archangel's trump, shall be as shadows past."

IV.

The Blessing of a Cheerful Piety.

There are briers besetting every path,
   That call for patient care;
There are trials and griefs in every lot,
   And a need for earnest prayer —
But a lowly heart that leans on Thee,
   Is happy everywhere.

AS long as everything goes prosperously with us, no losses nor calamities, no sickness nor death, nor unusual exposure to death of those we love, it is not a difficult thing to be cheerful, light-hearted and happy. It is very easy, under such circumstances, to rebuke the questionings and murmurings of those over whom the great water-floods of affliction have rolled; and who, in spite of all their faith, cannot keep back the anguish-cry of the Saviour, — "My God, my God! why hast thou forsaken me."

But let any of this class suddenly come into any kind of trouble; let some business misfortune bring them front to front with comparative poverty; or disease, attended with great bodily suffering, fall to their lot; or death strike down some beloved member of the family circle — oh, then it is quite another thing. They can be very eloquent in urging upon others the lesson of trust and resignation under affliction; but when *they* go down into the deeps, then it is their sorrow, and not another's. Then they talk very differently, and feel far otherwise than when the evil came to some acquaintance or neighbor, or even some friend. They learn the truth of the saying so often repeated, that it is easier always to bear other people's troubles than to bear one's own. Indeed, it is always easier to commend faith and submission to others, than to realize the blessing in our own souls. And yet the realization of this blessing in our own souls, is not an impossible thing. It is the product, largely, of Christian doctrine and knowledge, of Christian effort and culture. It is the harvest-sheaves of wheat which all can sow, since God has placed the rich seed grain within reach of all.

I do not intend by this universal phrasing of the thought, to be understood as saying there are not original and constitutional differences in men in regard to this matter. All men are not alike in their religious and moral structure, any more than in their mental capacities, or in bodily strength and size. The Creator has made them different. Two men, of equal spiritual life and culture, having the same theological belief, the same confident faith in the Divine direction of all human affairs, will not bear the same trouble with the same serenity and uncomplaining patience — and only because in physical constitution, in nervous irritability, they are wholly unlike; created unlike in the beginning, and not so because of any spiritual training by the one, or any neglect of it by the other.

Now, one of these men will face a great misfortune, or bear a long and painful sickness, or meet death with firmness and composure; and those beholding him set him down as a model Christian, a perfect religious man. The other will be overcome by these trials, he will bow to them as a reed in the wind; his courage fails him, his nerves betray him, the physical man, the sensitive body, in its tremor and weakness conquers the spirit, and his words and manner convince the superficial observer that he is wholly wanting in faith and trust toward God, in religious life and personal piety.

And yet nothing could be farther from the truth. It is not the man's faith or piety that are at fault, but his nerves, his excessively delicate and irritable physical constitution, played upon and swayed hither and thither by bodily pains or mental troubles, as the leaves of the forest are seized and swept to and fro by the fickle winds. I knew intimately a man of this sort, years ago, now in heaven. He was possessed of an excellent mind, cultivated by extensive reading, as truly Christian in life and spirit as any one I ever ministered to. But he was of a most sensitive temperament, extremely nervous, and keenly alive to every disturbing influence.

It is easy to see how a protracted and very painful disease would affect such a person. And the last days of his life were clouded to many of his friends (not to me who knew him so well,) by exhibitions of fretful impatience, complaints and accusations, and an absence of that confidence and reconciliation to the Divine will, which his previous life authorized us to expect. But with a nervous system utterly shattered by his sufferings, I knew all this was to be set down against the physical and not against the spiritual man. Other men, with not half his faith or piety, but with nerves of wrought iron, had met their trial with twice the courage and steadiness. I knew the soul was not faithless, but only that it could not control the quivering nerves, nor master the anguish of the frail and sensitive body. And we could see this in the seasons of lengthened relief and quiet, when the spirit was lifted for a moment out of the bodily wreck, and uttered itself in the old familiar dialect of holy trust and sweetest resignation.

Let those, therefore, who are gifted with strong nerves, as well as blessed with strong faith, be patient with such as are overwhelmed by their troubles, remembering the words of Paul, — "For who maketh thee to differ from another? and what hast thou that thou didst not receive? now if thou didst receive it, why dost thou glory, as if thou hadst not received it? .... Therefore judge nothing before the time, until the Lord come, who both will bring to light the hidden things of darkness, and will make manifest the counsels of the hearts; and then shall every man have praise of God." — 1 Cor. iv.

But we must be careful not to justify our impatience and complaint by forcing this view of the subject to an extreme. A just allowance should certainly be made for constitutional differences among men; for an original endowment, in one case, of strength and endurance entirely independent of faith and piety, and in another, for a frail and nerveless body, which is forever dragging the soul down into its own helplessness and gloom. Still we must not forget that, with multitudes having equal original gifts and opportunities, the results are widely different — and this from neglect of religious culture, from want of self-government, from cherishing an unhappy, dissatisfied and querulous temper.

Giving to the exceptions named their full weight in the explanation, it is nevertheless true that faith and piety, and the discipline of a Christian spirit and character, are a most important help to us in the day of trial — in misfortunes, in sickness, in bereavement, in our own death. It is nevertheless true that we can lighten our burthens, or otherwise, just according to the spirit in which we accept them. The same sickness or trouble to one person, fretful, resistant, disposed to see every thing, every event, on the wrong side, having no living faith in Providence, will press on him as with the weight of a mountain; but to another cheerful, patient, trying to make the best of everything, trying to see God in everything, it will be only as a handful of feathers.

It is the part of true wisdom, therefore, to cultivate a cheerful, hopeful disposition. By always looking on the dark side, and hunting up evil things, a man can soon change the order of his thoughts, can soon beget a sour and disagreeable temper, and make himself as unhappy as he is offensive to others, and unjust to his Maker. On the other hand, the man who is always seeking for sunny spots, for green grass and flowers, is sure to find them; and to find, also, that the light and fragrance will creep, by some subtle process, into all the shadows of his heart — till by and by his whole life comes out into the sunshine, in spite of his misfortunes and sorrows.

The truth is, there is always sunshine somewhere. There is always something to be thankful for, even in the darkest life. We should never let the taking away of one blessing, however precious, blind us to the value of those that are left. We should not forget in the sickness of to-day, the many days and years in which we have enjoyed perfect health, and been free from pain, and able to go about our daily duties without fatigue or suffering. How few the days of storm and rain, compared with those that are calm and sunny. How short the seasons of bodily distress and anguish, contrasted with the long periods of ease and comfort. We should think of this more than we do. It would teach us patience and resignation. If we count the days in which we are absolutely miserable, we shall be surprised to find how few they are compared with our complaints. And if we faithfully register every day in the year which brings us some sweetness, some enjoyment or some comfort, we shall feel rebuked for our many unjust accusations against our Heavenly Father, when we find how near the register comes to three hundred and sixty-five!

That was the true spirit of gratitude and submission exhibited by an aged saint, who in his poverty thanked God for a crust of bread, and the hope of heaven beside; and who, when pitied for his unprotected loneliness, replied, "I am never alone; Faith shuts my door at night, and Mercy opens it in the morning." It is wonderful how a pleasant disposition will lighten our burthens, and sweeten the wormwood of life. It is very beautiful, even when we are despondent ourselves, to see how the gloom of a sick chamber is sometimes illumined by the light of a cheerful piety, which will not let go its hold on God. The obscurest sufferer in this way becomes transfigured as with the glory of the Lord, and his faith and patience and sweet humility come to us with a ministry of reproof for our ingratitude toward Him, who has said for our encouragement and comfort, "I will never leave thee nor forsake thee?"

A truly religious spirit takes up this promise of the Lord, and, in sickness and affliction, makes it the rod and the staff whereon it leans; and by help of which it is rested and comforted, in its weary walk through the valley of shadows. But, as said, this spirit of reverent submission and affectionate confidence toward God, is not the product of a miracle wrought in the soul by the Holy Spirit; but the fruitage of seed which we ourselves must sow. Some effort is needed on our part. The promise of peace is conditional upon our seeking it. Without a knowledge of God we cannot trust him; and knowledge is the reward of labor, of study. If we never seek, we shall never find. "Ask, and ye shall receive; seek, and ye shall find; knock, and it shall be opened unto you."

Knowledge of God and of his love for us comes first, and then confidence in his wise and beneficent direction of all our troubles and trials; and then, a calm and cheerful resignation to his will; and then, an abiding peace which no sorrow, no evil can disturb — these are the natural sequences, linking into each other as cause and effect.

What can these anxious cares avail,
   These never-ceasing moans and sighs?
What can it help us to bewail
   Each painful moment as it flies?
Our cross and trials do but press
The heavier for our bitterness.

Leave God to order all thy ways,
   And hope in him whate'er betide;
Thoul't find him in the evil days
   Thy all sufficient strength and guide.
Who trusts in God's unchanging love,
Builds on the rock that nought can move.

V.

Is thy House in Order?

Lord may I be ready when death shall come,
May I be ready to hasten home!
No earthward clinging, no lingering gaze,
No strife at parting, no sore amaze;
No flitting shadows to dim the light
Of angel pinions winged for the flight;
No cloud-like phantoms to fling a gloom
'Twixt heaven's bright portals and earth's dark tomb —
But sweetly, gently, to pass away
From the world's dim twilight into day.

WE ought always to live in such way as to be prepared for whatever the day may bring forth. Not that we should ever be living in the shadow of death, or in constant expectation of sickness or calamity of any sort; but with wise regard to the possibility of misfortune, sickness, bereavement or death, at any moment. If we keep this in mind, and reflect upon it as a possibility at any time, as a certainty some time, we shall be careful to set our house in order, and so dispose our spiritual and temporal affairs, that we shall never be surprised or alarmed, however sudden the event.

This present sickness of yours has come upon you perhaps quite unexpectedly. Doubtless, could you have foreseen it, you would have finished many things now left incomplete; you would have brought your business into more compact form, arranged your papers, balanced your books, and gathered up all the loose threads in the web of your plans and purposes, which this sudden sickness has sadly entangled and deranged.

You do not know, no one can tell you, how this sickness will terminate. It may be that God, in his gracious mercy, will give you safe recovery; and it may be that, in equal mercy, he will call you to bid the world a final adieu. At any rate, if you recover from this sickness, you step back from the open grave only to approach it again in a few years, or a few months, perhaps.

Are you prepared for either issue? Is the soul ready for the change, strong in its faith, clear in its vision? Have you no errors to correct? no wrongs to redress? no shortcomings to regret? no sins to repent of? are your worldly affairs disposed according to your wishes? are there no last things you desire to do? no last words of direction and counsel you need to speak? In a word: Is your house in order? If so, then happy are you, for no sickness can surprise you into confusion; and death, however sudden, cannot alarm you.

There is no duty a man owes to himself, or to his family and those who love him, so sacred and binding as this perfect preparedness for sudden sickness and death. Since we never know when they may come, we should never be in any other than a state of readiness to meet them. The true Christian proves himself such by being ever ready, ever prepared in all respects, whether as regards himself, those dependent on him, or the world at large. He lives every day mindful of the fact that he may be prostrated by disease, or come to his death by some sudden calamity; and therefore, for this very reason, passes through life cheerfully and composedly, knowing that he *is* ready, ready to live or to die, as to the Lord may seem best.

Therefore, in the fitting words of Zschokke, " Prepare thy soul that it may be ready to depart at any moment; and see to it that thou fulfil day by day every duty toward those dependent on thee, and toward thy fellow-men. Do not flatter thyself with the hope that thou wilt have time during a long and lingering illness to put thy house in order.

" Who knows what his end may be? Who can in any way foretell whether he may not be cut off by some untoward accident? Therefore, prepare thy house, keep thy domestic affairs, thy worldly concerns, in order, so that, if thou be called away suddenly from the midst of thy friends, everything shall be found after thy dissolution arranged with such perfect care, that there shall be no neglected parts, no confusion. The praise of the living will follow thee; the blessings of thy loved ones will reach thee in the eternal abodes; thou wilt have fulfilled one of the most sacred duties towards those who are bound to thee by the ties of blood. We may always take it for granted, that he who kept his domestic affairs in order was found prepared in those more important matters also that lay between him and God. Live and act each day so that after thy death, were it even to take place the next minute, thy family shall not be left in want, and no blame shall attach to thy name. For the good name of the departed must ever be the most blessed inheritance to those he leaves behind. Arrange thy affairs so that they may at any moment be laid before the eyes of strangers, as is always more or less the case after our demise.

"Prepare thy house! If thou leadest at all

times a life of piety, innocence, benevolence, full of active well-doing, and free from hatred or anger, such as Jesus thy Saviour taught thee, then sudden death can only be to thee a sudden benefit. Why shouldst thou dread to appear before God? Art thou not ever in his presence? Hast thou not been, even from thy birth, one of his children, whom he holds in his arms, whom he watches over and protects? He knows thy short-comings; but he knows also thy earnest efforts to correct them. He sees also the honest fight which, in order to be worthy of him, thou fightest against the temptations to sin; he sees how often thou hast resisted and overcome thy tendencies to avarice or sensual enjoyment; he witnesses thy endeavors to make amends for every fault by noble actions. Ought a child to fear to appear before its loving parent, even though it have not yet conquered all its faults? Has not Jesus revealed to us the infinite mercy of the Father in all its beauty? Has he not given us assurances of his grace and his forgiveness?"

Fear not, then; but diligently ordering all thy worldly affairs, and walking after the example, and in the spirit, of thy Lord and Master, be prepared and waiting for the voice of the Lord. The measure of thy duties filled, the work given thee finished, the lessons of earth all learned, thou wilt be ready, when that voice comes to thee, to answer as the "child Samuel" answered to the heavenly call — "Here am I; speak, Lord, for thy servant heareth."

> The bird let loose in Eastern skies,
>   Returning fondly home,
> Ne'er stoops to earth her wing, nor flies
>   Where idle warblers roam;
> But high she shoots through air and light,
>   Above all low delay,
> Where nothing earthly bounds her flight,
>   Nor shadow dims her way
>
> So grant me, God, from every snare
>   Of sinful passion free,
> Aloft through faith's serener air
>   To hold my course to thee —
> No sin to cloud, no lure to stay
>   My soul, as home she springs;
> Thy sunshine on her joyful way,
>   Thy freedom on her wings.

VI.

Inspired Meditations for the Sick Chamber.

O Father, — draw me after thee,
  So shall I run and never tire;
Thy presence still my comfort be,
  My hope, my joy, my sole desire;
Thy spirit grant; — for neither fear
Nor sin can come, while that is near.

THE Lord is my light and my salvation; whom shall I fear? the Lord is the strength of my life; of whom shall I be afraid? For in the time of trouble he shall hide me in his pavilion: in the secret of his tabernacle shall he hide me; he shall set me upon a rock.

In thee, O Lord, do I put my trust. In

the day of trouble I will call upon thee, for thou wilt answer me. When I remember thee upon my bed, and meditate on thee in the night watches; How precious are thy thoughts unto me, O God! how great is the sum of them! If I should count them, they are more in number than the sand: when I awake, I am still with thee.

Thus will I bless thee while I live: I will lift up my hands in thy name. For thou Lord art good, and ready to forgive; and plenteous in mercy to all them that call upon thee.

O Lord God of my salvation, I have cried day and night before thee: Let my prayer come before thee; incline thine ear unto my cry; For my days are like a shadow that declineth; and I am withered like grass.

I am counted with those that go down to the grave; I am as a man that hath no strength: For thou hast laid me in the lowest pit, in darkness, and in the deeps. Thou hast afflicted me with all thy waves. Mine eye mourneth by reason of affliction: Lord I have called daily upon thee, I have stretched out my hands unto thee.

I am afflicted and ready to die: why hidest thou thy face from me? Look upon my affliction and my pain, and forgive all my sins.

Hear me, O Lord, for thy loving-kindness is good: turn unto me according to the multitude of thy mercies. And hide not thy face from thy servant; for my soul is full of troubles, and my life draweth nigh unto the grave.

Deep calleth unto deep at the noise of thy water-spouts: all thy waves and thy billows are gone over me.

———

Why art thou cast down, O my soul? and why art thou disquieted within me? hope thou in God: for I shall yet praise him who is the health of my countenance, and my God. For his anger endureth but a moment; but in his favor is life: weeping may endure for a night, but joy cometh in the morning.

I know, O Lord, that thy judgments are right; and that in faithfulness thou hast afflicted me. Therefore will I not fear, for I know in whom I have believed, and am persuaded that he is able to keep that which I have committed unto him.

The Lord hath chastened me sore; but he hath not given me over to death. Therefore I shall not die, but live, and declare the works of the Lord.

I will go into thy house with praise offerings: I will pay thee my vows, which my lips have uttered, and my mouth hath spoken, when I was in trouble.

So wilt thou recover me, and make me to live. For the grave cannot praise thee, death cannot celebrate thee. What profit is there in my life when I go down to the grave? Shall the dust praise thee? shall it declare thy truth? The living, the living, he shall praise thee, as I do this day: the father to the children shall make known thy truth.

Nevertheless, O Father! if this cup may

not pass from me except I drink it, thy will be done. The cup which my Father hath given me, shall I not drink it? The spirit indeed is willing, but the flesh is weak. The flesh and the heart faileth, but God is the strength of my heart, and my portion forever.

The Lord is my shepherd; I shall not want. He maketh me to lie down in green pastures; he leadeth me beside the still waters. He restoreth my soul; he leadeth me in the paths of righteousness for his name's sake. Yea, though I walk through the Valley of the Shadow of Death, I will fear no evil; for Thou art with me: thy rod and thy staff they comfort me.

I am continually with thee: thou hast holden me by my right hand. Thou shalt guide me with thy counsels, and afterward receive me to glory. Therefore return unto thy rest, O my soul; for the Lord hath dealt bountifully with thee.

VII.

Divine Consolations for the Sick.

In suffering be thy love my peace;
In weakness be thy grace my power;
And when the storms of life shall cease,
O God! in that important hour,
In death as life be thou my guide,
And bear me through its whelming tide.

HUMBLE yourselves under the mighty hand of God, that he may exalt you in due time; Casting all your care upon him, for he careth for you. Like as a father pitieth his children, so the Lord pitieth them that fear him. For he knoweth our frame; he remembereth that we are dust.

His eyes are upon the ways of man; he seeth all his goings; and he will not lay upon man more than is right. Though he cause grief, yet will he have compassion according to the multitude of his mercies. For he doth not afflict willingly, nor grieve the children of men.

They that sow in tears shall reap in joy. He that goeth forth and weepeth, bearing precious seed, shall doubtless come again with rejoicing, bringing his sheaves with him.

Beloved, think it not strange concerning the fiery trial which is to try you, as though some strange thing happened unto you: But rejoice, inasmuch as ye are partakers of Christ's sufferings, that when his glory is revealed, ye may be glad also with exceeding joy.

Despise not the chastening of the Lord; neither be weary of his correction: For whom the Lord loveth he correcteth; even as a father the son in whom he delighteth. No chastening for the present seemeth to be joyous, but grievous; nevertheless it afterward yieldeth the peaceable fruits of righteousness to them that are exercised thereby. For I reckon that the sufferings of this present time are not worthy to be compared with the glory which shall be revealed in us.

It is the Lord, let him do what seemeth to him good. In a dream, in a vision of the night, when deep sleep falleth upon men, in slumberings upon the bed; Then he openeth the ears of men, and sealeth their instruction, that he may withdraw man from his purpose, and hide pride from man.

He chasteneth him also with pain upon his bed, and the multitude of his bones with strong pain; So that his life abhorreth bread, and his soul dainty meat. His flesh is consumed away, that it cannot be seen; and his bones that were not seen stick out. Yea, his soul draweth near unto the grave, and his life to destruction.

If there be a messenger with him, an interpreter, one among a thousand, to show man his uprightness; Then is he gracious unto him, and saith, Deliver him from going down to the grave: I have found a ransom.

His flesh shall be fresher than a child's: he shall return to the days of his youth: He shall pray unto God, and he will be favorable unto him; and he shall see his face with joy; for he will render unto man his righteousness. He keepeth back his soul from the grave, and his life from perishing. Lo, all these things worketh God oftentimes with man. It is good, therefore, that a man should both hope and quietly wait for the salvation of the Lord.

Call upon me in the day of trouble: I will deliver thee, and thou shalt glorify me. I will strengthen thee; yea, I will help thee; yea, I will uphold thee with the right hand of my righteousness.

Then shalt thou lift up thy face without spot; yea, thou shalt be steadfast, and shalt not fear. Because thou shalt forget thy misery, and remember it only as waters that pass away.

And thou shalt be secure, because there is

hope; thou shalt take thy rest in safety; When thou liest down, thou shalt not be afraid; yea, thou shalt lie down, and thy sleep shall be sweet: For he giveth his beloved sleep; the Lord shall give thee rest from thy sorrow.

Behold the fowls of the air, for they sow not, neither do they reap, nor gather into barns; yet your heavenly Father feedeth them. Are ye not much better than they? Are not five sparrows sold for two farthings, and not one of them is forgotten before God? But even the very hairs of your head are all numbered. Fear not, therefore; ye are of more value than many sparrows.

Come unto me all ye that labor and are heavy laden, and I will give you rest. Take my yoke upon you, and learn of me, for I am meek and lowly in heart; and ye shall find rest unto your souls. For my yoke is easy, and my burden is light.

Peace I leave with you, my peace I give unto you: not as the world giveth, give I unto you. Let not your heart be troubled, neither let it be afraid.

For to this end Christ died, and rose, and revived, that he might be Lord both of the dead and the living. For none of us liveth to himself, and no man dieth to himself. For whether we live, we live unto the Lord; and whether we die, we die unto the Lord: whether we live therefore or die, we are the Lord's.

For we know that, if our earthly house of this tabernacle were dissolved, we have a building of God, a house not made with hands, eternal in the heavens. For which cause we faint not; for though our outward man perish, yet the inward man is renewed day by day: For our light affliction, which is but for a moment, worketh for us a far more exceeding and eternal weight of glory.

For this corruptible must put on incorruption, and this mortal must put on immortality. And as we have borne the image of the earthy, we shall also bear the image of the heavenly.

And God shall wipe away all tears, and there shall be no more death, neither sorrow, nor crying, neither shall there be any more pain; for the former things are passed away!

Revelations for the Dying.

Yea, though I walk through the Valley of the Shadow of Death, I will fear no evil, for thou art with me; thy rod and thy staff they comfort me.—Psalm xxiii. 4.

Over the river they beckon to me —
  Loved ones who've crossed to the further side;
The gleam of their snowy robes I see,
  But their voices are drowned by the dashing tide.

And none return from those quiet shores,
  Who cross with the boatman cold and pale;
We hear the dip of the golden oars,
  And catch a gleam of the snowy sail,
And lo! they have passed from the yearning heart,
  They cross the stream, and are gone for aye;
We may not sunder the veil apart
  That hides from our vision the gates of day;
We only know that their barques no more
  May sail with ours o'er life's stormy sea;
Yet somewhere I know, on the unseen shore,
  They watch, and beckon, and wait for me.

And I sit and think when the sunset's gold
  Is flushing river, and hill, and shore,
I shall one day stand by the water cold,
  And list for the sound of the boatman's oar:
I shall watch for a gleam of the flapping sail;
  I shall hear the boat as it gains the strand;
I shall pass from sight with the boatman pale
  To the better shores of the spirit-land.

I shall know the loved who have gone before,
  And joyfully sweet will the meeting be,
When over the river, the peaceful river,
  The angel of Death shall carry me.

I.

"Over the River."

And we only know, when we hear no more,
   As we watch for the parting breath,
That an angel is tenderly lifting them down
   The banks of the river of death —
Only know that their footsteps are pressing the sands
   That are washed by the hurrying waves,
And that over the billows outstretched are their hands,
   To the shore that their brightness laves.

ONE of the most beautiful metaphors by which we represent the passage from this world to another, is that embodied in the title of this little volume — OVER THE RIVER. It is not afar off, that other world; it is not beyond the waste wilderness of space, hidden in the invisible abysses of the heavens — but it is near to us, close at hand; just over the river, and we are there!

And the way to it is not long. It may sometimes be toilsome; it may have difficult places, and the flinty rock and the sharp thorn may sometimes tear the tender feet. But the *River* is not distant — at the longest, the way does not stretch much beyond threescore and ten or fourscore miles. And then, when our strength fails, we embark for the land of rest; we are borne across the river, and almost ere we know it, we are stepping forth upon the green shores of the land of the immortals. And then, rested and refreshed, our burthens laid aside, our youth renewed, what a world of beauty, what a life of joy opens before us!

And there are our companions too, they who crossed the river before us; the beloved, the beautiful, who wait for us on the other shore. Knowing of our coming, they leave all else to come down to the river's bank, that they may be the first to welcome us to the land of the blessed, the home of the children of God. They have wandered over the green fields, and through the rose-wreathed bowers, and along the winding paths, and the hillsides bright with flowers; they have breathed the pure airs, and rejoiced in the delicious melodies, of the Lord's Paradise — and so they know what joys await us, what blessedness unspeakable will be ours and theirs together.

They will be the first, therefore, to greet us when we reach the other side — they who knew us and loved us here. And what a sweet surprise, what a new gladness to us, when first we open our eyes upon the realities of the spiritual world, to behold the dear faces of those who in this world were our heart's treasures, and who, when they went away, left such sorrow behind them. O the bliss of that meeting, the ecstasy of that welcome from the beloved over the river! How it takes from the sharp pain of parting with those who are *here*, when we know how soon we shall be with those who are *there*. And, how it soothes the bereaved and desolate heart to feel that the precious ones, who have gone, or are going, will find familiar spirits, dear friends, waiting for them on the heavenly shore, ready to lead them to the Saviour, and to walk with them through the many mansions of the Father's house.

Ah, how much it would narrow the river of death, how nigh to us it would bring the spirit land, and those who have passed the boundaries of time into the life immortal — if we could only come always to think and feel in this way. And it requires only that we should make our faith living and earnest as that of the early disciples, to have this blessing realized unto our souls. They believed in Jesus, and in the grand revelation of life illustrated and confirmed by his resurrection. They believed that the future hinged on to the present, and that the river which separates this world from the other, is of so little breadth, that the farther shore is almost visible from this side to the clear sight of Christian faith. And sometimes, when lifted up by the inspirations of this faith, and standing rapt on the mount of vision, they seemed for a moment to get actual sight of the green fields and purple hills of the heavenly country.

So it always is, or may be. Where there is true and living faith, there is spiritual vision. The Christian, who makes the teachings of the Saviour real, who incorporates into his inmost being the elements of his revelations, makes his truth the soul's bread of life, lays hold upon the doctrine of immortality — he is gifted thereby with a new power of spiritual sight. And, though he may not always be able to pierce through the mists which lie along the river of death, his soul is sometimes lifted above them, and he sees over and across, and gets glimpses of the splendors that stream up from the city of God, the heavenly Jerusalem.

It is not the peculiar gift of those who stood near to Jesus — this far sight to the green fields and the blessed abodes beyond the swelling flood. Not only the favored ones who listened to truth as it fell from his lips, but all his disciples, in all ages of the world, enjoy the same privilege. We of to-day, if we will appropriate the life-giving doctrines of the Saviour, and weave them up into the very texture of our souls, may take the blessing and the reward — for it is the reward of a diligent culture of the religious nature, of faith in Christ and the Gospel.

The beauties of the landscape are realities; they are there in all their substance and attractiveness — but only the eye of the artist, of the true lover and diligent student of nature, takes them all in, and detects the minute and delicate lines and touches which so largely make up the charm of the picture.

So the country over the river is a reality, a substantive glory; but the soul that can grasp it in thought and faith, must be trained to it by a true Christian life. The departed are there, radiant with happiness, rejoicing in the wondrous beauties of the heavenly Eden, coming down often to the very banks of the river, flinging flowers upon its flowing bosom, which sometimes drift over to our shore — but he who would look across to where they are, must accustom his eyes to this work. It is not the distance, but our own short-sightedness, the dimness of our vision that hinders us. We must clear our eyes of the film that the world has gathered upon them, we must strive to clarify the atmosphere on this side the river; and then, if not always, yet sometimes in our moments of exaltation, when the soul is lifted up by prayer or praise or spiritual communion, we may hope to catch sight of the heavenly heights beyond the river, and of the glorified forms of those who are "children of God, being children of the Resurrection."

This is what the apostle means, when he says "Faith is the substance of things hoped for, the evidence of things not seen" with the natural eye. He has spoken of the righteous men of the early times, the sainted souls who walked with God on earth; and then he adds in beautiful phrase — "These all died in faith, not having received the promises, but having seen them afar off, and were persuaded of them, and embraced them, and confessed that they were strangers and pilgrims on the earth. For they that say such things declare plainly that they seek a country. And truly, if they had been mindful of (desirous of, attached to) that country from whence they came out, they might have had opportunity to have returned. But now they desire a better country, that is an heavenly: wherefore God is not ashamed to be called their God, for he hath prepared for them a city." — Heb. xi.

These ancient worthies, far back in the dim twilight of the world's morning, seeing the promises imperfectly, afar off, still walked forward in faith, persuaded that the good God who had made them, had "provided for them some better thing" than this life had brought them. They did not comprehend the fulness of the blessing in store for them. The Sun of Righteousness had not risen upon them; and the mists and fogs which hung over the river were thick and heavy — and they could not see across. But they believed in the better country, and felt that they were only sojourners and strangers here, and, however feeble their vision, they still went forward with a patient courage, and died in the faith.

But with the Christian it is not early morning, but the noon of the day. With us it is no longer dim and "afar off;" but near unto us, and visible to the eye of perfect Christian faith. The "evidence" and the "substance" are ours — if we are true to our opportunities, and diligently use the appointed means for training and strengthening our spiritual sight. And if those saintly men of old so mastered the ills and sorrows of life, and came to the river's bank so calmly, with such sweet peace at the heart — O how ought it to be with us, who have seen the empty sepulchre of Jesus, and know the power of his Resurrection!

If these old patriarchs could trust in the promises, and "die in faith," what courage, what triumph should be ours who have the promises fulfilled unto us! What comfort, what confidence, what victory for us, since Jesus died that he might "deliver them who, through fear of death, were all their lifetime subject to bondage!"—Heb. ii.

And often I sit at the casement alone,
   And I list, if perchance I may hear,
The flutter of sails, and the rushing of waves,
   And the dash of a gilded oar,
As the boatman starts from his emerald caves
   To carry me down to the shore —
And I wait for the swoop of an angel wing,
   And the clasp of an angel hand,
For the sound of a harp and the chant of a hymn,
   And the light of the glory land.

But, alas! I listen and wait in vain;
   Yet I know that my weary feet
Shall wander ere long from the valley of pain,
   To the river so solemn and sweet.
I shall go with the boatman, changeless and pale,
   And each woe that my heart has known,
Each agonized cry, each desolate wail,
   Each fearful and piteous moan,
Shall be swept away by the murmurous waves,
   From my spirit so joyous and free,
When I see the smiles of the lovely who wait
   On the beautiful shore for me.

II.

The Earthly Tent—the Heavenly House.

I know not the way I am going,
  But well do I know my Guide;
With a childlike trust I give my hand
  To the mighty Friend by my side.

'Tis home, 'tis home, that we wish to reach;
  He who guides us may choose the way;
For little we heed what path we take,
  If we're nearer *home* each day.

A FREQUENT and pleasing figure or metaphor of the Scriptures, is that which represents mankind as sojourners or temporary dwellers on earth, having their home or permanent residence in heaven. David, in his prayer to the Lord, says, "All things come of Thee, and of thine own have we given Thee. For we are strangers before Thee, and sojourners, as were all our fathers: our days on earth are as a shadow, and there is none abiding." — 1 Chronicles xxix. And Peter says, "If ye call on the Father, who without respect of persons judgeth according to every man's work, pass the time of your sojourning here in fear;" that is, reverently toward this Father. Then there were the ancient saints who "confessed that they were strangers and pilgrims on the earth."

This figure furnishes abundant subject matter for meditation, and presents a pleasing and consoling truth to the thought of the sufferer, and of those who have seen their beloved pass on out of their sight. This is not our home — we are away from home in this world. We are travellers, sojourning here and there, on the way to the country beyond the river, our native land, from which we went out at birth. "We have no continuing city here, but we seek one to come;" as did the old patriarch, who "sojourned in the land of promise, as in a strange country, dwelling in tabernacles with Isaac and Jacob, the heirs with him of the same promise — for he looked for a city which hath foundations, whose maker and builder is God."

We should seek to be in this frame of mind, to feel with Abraham that we are pilgrims in this foreign land, journeying forward every day toward a city having foundations, the New Jerusalem on high. We ought to make this a subject of frequent thought, and cheerfully look forward to the time when we shall go to take possession of our heavenly mansion — or in the language of the apostle, when we shall "come unto mount Sion, and unto the city of the living God, the heavenly Jerusalem, and to an innumerable company of angels, and to the general assembly and Church of the first-born, which are written in heaven, and to God the Judge of all, and to the spirits of just men made perfect, and to Jesus the mediator of the new covenant."

What a glorious company, indeed, ready to

receive us, and give us welcome when we come into that beautiful land wherein we are to abide forever. It is something, truly, to look forward to, to be glad for; something to give courage and strength as we travel on through the pleasant valleys, or the waste wilderness, or over the rough mountain passes of life. It is a sweet and soothing thought, that every day is one remove nearer to the mansions of the Blessed, where all our journeyings shall end in the dear quiet of home; where all the saints of earth and of heaven, and all the great and good of all ages and all worlds, are waiting to greet us with rejoicings, to embrace us in the arms of everlasting love.

Tired with our long travel, fainting with hunger and thirst, the hot sun of the desert blazing upon us, O how grateful to the sinking frame is the sight of the green and shady palms, that lift their tall plumes along the horizon, and discover to us the boundaries, the end at last, of the great sand waste; the region of grass and flowers and fruits and running waters, the shady nook in which nestles "the sweet, sweet home," where we shall find rest and peace, and all the joys of tenderest affection forevermore. Some one has said in pleasant phrase, and to be remembered by all, —

> "Here in the body pent,
> Absent from heaven I roam,
> Yet nightly pitch my moving tent
> A day's march nearer home."

How beautiful, how comforting! Absent from heaven, from home, yet every night we are one day's march nearer to it; one day less between us and those we love, those who are waiting to welcome us to the city of God, and to bring us to the place of our rest.

And this leads to that beautiful passage of Paul in 2 Corinthians v. 1: "For we know that if our earthly house of this tabernacle (tent) were dissolved, we have a building of God, an house not made with hands, eternal in the heavens"— or substantially, "we know when our *temporary tent* of the body is struck on earth, we have from God an *eternal house*, not made with hands, in the heavens." The beauty and force of this passage is mostly lost in the common translation. The contrast which the apostle sets out is between a moveable tent and a permanent house; between a temporary sojourn, a journey, a pilgrimage on earth, and an eternal residence in heaven.

There is allusion to the ancient Jewish tabernacle, which was only a temporary abode, and which, whenever the Israelites moved from the place of their sojourning on the way to the promised land, was *dissolved*, or *taken in pieces*, and the ark of the covenant, covered with its own curtains, was carried forward by itself. The comparison is between this humble tabernacle or tent, thus taken to pieces and moved from station to station, and the splendid temple in which the sacred ark found a fixed and permanent abode.

So the body is the tabernacle, or tent, in which the spirit takes up its abode while on its journey to the promised land; and when this mortal habitation is dissolved, when the *tent* is struck by Death, then the soul is clothed upon with the immortal, and enters into its heavenly *house*, the building of God, where, its pilgrimage ended, it will dwell rejoicingly forevermore! Hence Paul says, "we desire to be clothed upon with our *house* which is from heaven; for we that are in this *tent* (tabernacle) do groan, being burdened; not that we would be unclothed, but clothed upon, that mortality may be swallowed up of life .... knowing that, whilst we are at home in the body, we are absent from the Lord — for we walk by faith and not by sight."

There is no metaphor in all the Bible more beautiful than this, or more full of comfort to the weary toiler, to the heart that has been bereaved, to the poor sufferer who with failing strength and trembling step is approaching the end of his Life pilgrimage. At home in the body we are absent from the Lord;

dwelling in tents we have no fixed habitation, we are travelling onward toward the city where our home is to be, where our kindred dwell, or will by and by come to join us. Here everything is transient, changing, temporary — there everything is permanent, fixed and final. Here we meet and part; to-day we are together rejoicing, and to-morrow we are scattered in sadness and tears. But there we are together always, no more separation nor sadness, we are *at home* in the many mansions of our Father's house. This thought of the Heavenly Home, and the transfer to it of one after another of the family circle, till all our heart's treasures are on the other side, finds beautiful expression in the following passage from "Athanasia, or Foregleams of Immortality:"

"*Our home is always where our affections are.* We sigh and wander, we vibrate to and fro, till we rest in that special centre where our deepest loves are garnered up. Then the heart fills and brims over with its own happiness, and spreads sweetness and fertility all around it. Very often when the eyes are closing in death, and this world is shutting off the light from the departing soul, the last wish which is made audible is 'to go home.' The words break out sometimes through the cloud of delirium; but it is the soul's deepest and most central want, groping after its object, haply soon to find it as the clogs of earth clear away, and she springs up on the line of swift affection, as the bee with unerring precision shoots through the dusk of evening to her cell.

"How admirable are the arrangements of Providence by which he gradually removes the home-centre from this world to the other, and so draws our affections towards the heavenly abodes! We start in life an unbroken company; brothers and sisters, friends and lovers, neighbors and comrades, are with us; there is circle within circle, and each one of us is at the charmed centre where the heart's affections are aglow, and whence they radiate outward upon society. Youth is exuberant with joy and hope, the earth looks fair, for it sparkles with May-dews wet, and no shadow hath fallen upon it. We are all here, and we could live here forever. The home-centre is on the hither side of the river, and why should we strain our eyes to look beyond? But this state of things does not continue long. Our circle grows less and less. It is broken and broken, and then closes up again; but every break and close make it narrower and smaller. Perhaps before the sun is at his meridian the majority are on the other side, the circle there is as large as the one here, and we are drawn contrariwise and vibrate between the two. A little longer, and we have almost all crossed over; the balance settles down on the spiritual side, and the home-centre is removed to the upper sphere."

O child of sorrow! cherish these pleasing and consoling thoughts. Take to your heart these gospel truths, and you shall find in them that peace which passeth knowledge, and abideth forever. If the benignant face and venerable form of a parent is missed from your fireside, if the beloved companion, the chosen of your affections, if any of the dear lambs of the flock, have left you, and passed on over the river; remember, they have only gone home, they have finished the journey of life, they have laid aside the worn and weather-beaten tent, and have entered into that "building of God, not made with hands, eternal in the heavens." No more wanderings for them, no more journeyings in the desert, no more faintness nor weariness. "They shall not hunger nor thirst; neither shall the heat nor the sun smite them; for he that hath mercy on them shall lead them, even by the springs of water shall he guide them." Henceforth, to every one of these foot-worn and drooping pilgrims, the words of the sweet singer of Israel will be realized: "The Lord is thy keeper, the Lord is thy shade upon thy right hand. The sun shall not smite thee by day, nor the moon by night. The Lord shall preserve thee from all evil: he shall preserve thy soul. The Lord shall direct thy going out and thy coming in, even forevermore."

And you, too, poor afflicted soul, upon whom the hand of suffering has been laid so heavily, wasting with consumption, devoured with fever, racked with convulsions, or frantic with the streaming anguish of nerves on fire; over whom the weary days and the long nights pass in sad procession, bringing no relief. O be patient, and brave, and hopeful — every setting sun brings you farther on your way through the burning sands; every night you pitch your frail and shattered tent "a day's march nearer home." Be patient and enduring, for the river is not far off now, and on its banks you may strike your tent for the last time; and, passing over to the other shore, you will be welcomed by the immortal spirits waiting to receive you, and to lead you to your heavenly habitation. And there "*God shall wipe away all tears from your eyes; and there shall be no more death, neither sorrow, nor crying, neither shall there be any more pain: for the former things are passed away.*"

> "Worn and weary, oft the pilgrim
>   Hails the setting of the sun;
> For his goal is one day nearer,
>   And his journey nearly done.
> Thus we feel when o'er life's desert,
>   Heart and sandal sore we roam;
> As the twilight gathers o'er us,
>   We are one day nearer home.
>
> "Nearer home! Yes, one day nearer
>   To our Father's house on high —
> To the green fields and the fountains
>   Of the land beyond the sky:
> For the heavens grow brighter o'er us,
>   And the lamps hang in the dome,
> And our tents are pitched still closer,
>   For we're one day nearer home."

III.

Falling Asleep.

With her eyelids closed and her lips apart,
    And her arms like the marble fair,
Crossed on her bosom, and gently prest,
She lay, as she sank to her peaceful rest,
    In the mute repose of prayer.
When the morning broke and we gazed again,
    A smile to her face seemed given;
And though our spirits were crushed and sad,
The Christmas bells soon made us glad,
    For we knew she woke in Heaven.

"FOR so he giveth his beloved sleep." The relation of death to sleep is recognised among all nations, in one form or another. Not unfrequently sleep is made the symbol of death; and sometimes it is designated by that name. This is the case both in the Old and New Testament scriptures, more especially in the New. "For the maid is not dead, but sleepeth;" "our friend Lazarus sleepeth;" "them who sleep in Jesus will God bring with him;" "we shall not all sleep, but we shall all be changed;" "when Stephen had said this, he fell asleep;" "part remain, but some are fallen asleep." "Since the fathers fell asleep, all things continue as they were."

This figure is a very beautiful one, and not without its comforting associations. How grateful to the worn and tired worker, on whom the heat and burthen of the day have fallen with exhausting power, is the coming on of the evening, the hour of rest and repose. How welcome to the fainting traveller whose weary feet have trodden the dusty highway from the early light of morning, whose strength is well nigh spent, whose trembling limbs refuse to bear him farther — how welcome to his longing eyes is the sight of the little wayside inn, where he can rest from his long journey, and lie down and sleep — *sleep* till the body is refreshed, and its strength renewed — and then, when the morning comes, wake again to new life, and activity, and enjoyment.

To many a weary toiler in the field of the World, to many a fainting traveller on the high-road of life, this figure, which makes death a sleep, and the grave the couch on which we lie down to rest, comes with a peculiar and not unpleasant meaning.

I knew one whose life had been shadowed with sorrow, who for years had struggled with bitter memories, and domestic trials, and harsh treatment, and all the straitening ills of poverty, who held to this thought of death and the hereafter with singular tenacity of faith and feeling. At last her griefs were too heavy for the exhausted mind and body to bear. She began rapidly to sink under them — and then her thoughts dwelt perpetually on this idea of death, and she talked of little else. Her only thought of heaven was that she should rest and be at peace. "O how sweet it will be to *sleep*, to be at *rest* —

no more to suffer, nor to toil; no more weariness and exhaustion — to fall into placid, refreshing slumber, to rest undisturbed, and then to wake, and still to *rest;* to be free from care and pain, no more anguish of mind or heart; to dwell in everlasting peace and tranquility! I welcome the hour when, falling asleep in Jesus, I shall wake in that heavenly home, "where the wicked cease from troubling, and the weary are at rest."

So have others felt, poor sufferers, to whom life has been a scene of incessant toil, or of mental anxieties and struggles. Many a one has seen his cherished hopes blasted, his affections laid waste, and all the beauty and worth of life swept away from him by a series of fast following calamities and griefs; till at last, worn out, nerveless, broken in spirit, the prospect of a termination to these long continued trials is grateful to the crushed heart, and the sleep of death is looked forward to with almost longing.

And then there are those who, all their life

long, have maintained perpetual struggle with temptations and their own weaknesses and passions; who have striven for a nobler and better life, and have earnestly prayed, and wrestled with evil, and sought with all their energies to rise up into the heavenly life of holiness and triumphant virtue — but, failing in every effort, falling as often as they have risen, dragged down by the hounds of appetite, hindered and oppressed, yielding and unresisting, have finally, after every unsuccessful effort, sunk down again into the old life of weakness and sin. O what unspeakable relief to these is the thought, that by and by the long warfare will be ended, the last battle fought, and, laying off the dusty armor of conflict, they will lie down and *sleep* — no more temptation nor struggle, no more vain efforts and failures, no more heart-sickness and discouragement and despair; but rest from all this, rest in tranquil slumber through the quiet night — and at last, through the help of Jesus, disentangled from the earthly and corruptible, and by the grace of God renewed in the image of the heavenly, to rise when the morning comes, and go forth in the freedom and joy of the spiritual life!

And you, poor toilers, sinking with fatigue, worn in body, the fever burning through your veins; yet, remembering those at home and the wants that beset them, bending to your task while strength lasts — O be patient and cheerful, be of good heart, for the sun is in the west, the evening approaches when your task will be complete, and, casting aside the implements of labor, you may lie down and sink into the arms of profound, refreshing sleep!

And you who in close garrets ply with weary fingers the fast flying needle, far into the night, while the hot head throbs with sharp pains, and the exhausted body trembles with weakness and overwork, and consumption eats in upon the secret stores of life; who, day by day, and night by night, feel that your strength is growing less, and your toil more difficult, and the anguish of brain and heart more dreadful; and who long for the sweet privilege of rest and sleep, for the undreaming and renewing slumbers of childhood — be comforted in your sorrow, faint not in your weariness, for only a little longer, and the busy fingers, and the throbbing head and anxious heart, will be at rest. A little longer, and those heavy eyelids shall close over the tear-dimmed eyes, and the weary brain fall asleep and be at peace. A little longer, and you shall cease from your labors, and tranquilly fold your arms to rest — and nothing shall disturb your slumbers till the voice of the angel calls to you, and you wake in the likeness of God, wake to participate in the everlasting peace and blessedness of Heaven.

To you, therefore, and to all who are walking in weariness, oppressed with the burthen of their sorrows, or fainting with excess of toil, or discouraged by the long fight with temptation; this metaphor, which makes of death a sleep, and of the grave a bed of rest, is one full of sweet and welcome associations. It brings thoughts soothing and quieting to the worn and worried heart, and breathes a serene and tranquilizing influence upon the sad and fainting spirit. It is a blessed thing to sleep when we are so utterly prostrated. It is an unspeakable relief to fling the weary body down upon the couch of rest, feeling that we shall be left to slumber on undisturbed, till all fatigue and exhaustion have left us; till nature wakens us invigorated, restored, with new strength and vitality coursing through all the veins, and streaming along all the electric nerves of life.

And so the Holy Spirit, which is the Comforter, has chosen this beautiful figure wherewith to clothe the idea of death, that it may suggest cheerful and pleasant thoughts to the weary and tired children of earth; that it may help them to walk forward with a serene trust to the place of their rest, assured that when the morning comes, they will awake refreshed, quickened with new life and energy, the "children of God, being children of the Resurrection!"

My hands are weary, laboring, toiling on,
   Day after day for perishable meat:
Oh, city of our God, I fain would rest;
   I sigh to gain thy glorious mercy-seat.

My garments, travel-worn and stained with dust,
   Oft rent by briers and thorns that crowd my way,
Would fain be made, O Lord my righteousness,
   Spotless and white in heaven's unclouded ray.

My heart is weary of its frequent sin —
   Sinning, repenting, sinning still alway:
When shall my soul thy glorious presence feel,
   And find its guilt, dear Saviour, washed away?

Patience, poor soul: the Saviour's feet were worn;
   The Saviour's heart and hands were weary too;
His garments stained and travel-worn and old,
   His sacred eyes blinded with tears for you.

Love thou the path of sorrow that he trod;
   Toil on, and wait in patience for thy rest:
O city of our God, we soon shall see
   Thy glorious walls, home of the loved and blest.

IV.

The Death of the Body the Life of the Spirit.

"There's no such thing as death:" —
In nature nothing dies,
From each sad remnant of decay,
Some forms of life arise.

"There's no such thing as death:" —
'Tis but the blossom spray
Sinking before the coming fruit
That seeks the Summer's ray; —
'Tis but the bud displaced
As comes the perfect flower;
'Tis faith exchanged for sight,
And weariness for power.

ANOTHER significant metaphor, prophetic of the condition into which Death introduces the soul, is found in the following from 1 Corinthians xv. 36–38:

"That which thou sowest is not quickened except it die; and that which thou sowest, thou sowest not that body that shall be, but bare grain, it may chance of wheat, or some other grain, but God giveth it a body as it hath pleased him, and to every seed his own body."

The main idea of this metaphor is too plainly stated by the apostle to be mistaken. It is the same which the Saviour uttered in almost the same words in John xii. 24: "Verily, verily, I say unto you, except a corn of wheat fall into the ground and die, it abideth alone; but if it die, it bringeth forth much fruit." And this saying of his was in reference to his own death and resurrection, as the type, and the pledge, of the resurrection of mankind; of the deliverance of the whole race from the bondage of corruption into the glorious liberty of the incorruptible and immortal.

The thought set out by this metaphor, the beautiful truth which it presents, is worthy of special consideration, both for its theological importance, and for its comforting power in the most momentous hour of the soul's earthly history.

Planted in the ground the sheath or body of the seed begins at once the process of dissolution, or begins to die; and the moment the process of death commences in the outward body of the seed, "it may chance of wheat or any other grain," that same moment the process of the new birth commences with the interior germ. Nay, the death of the outer tegument or covering is absolutely necessary to this renewing process of the soul of the seed; the life of the one is the product of the other's death. And the substance of the decaying body becomes the means of developing the hitherto dormant powers of the germ; the medium by which it receives or appropriates to itself the subtle forces of the soil, the elements of its growth into new and larger life. If the body did not die, the germ could not be quickened, as the apostle says. It is only when the outer covering moulders away, that the external influences are able to reach the latent rudiments of the new life that is to be.

And one cannot but be struck with amazement, when he carefully considers the matter, to see what vast and astonishing powers, capacities and resources, lie folded up in a single grain of corn or wheat; and which by the decomposition of the body are, as it were, loosed from their prison, and set free to act.

In 1660 Sir Kenelm Digby saw a plant of barley, proceeding from a single grain, from which there came two hundred and forty-nine stalks, on which he counted upwards of eighteen thousand grains! But this is little compared with the experiments recorded in 58th vol. of the Philosophical Transactions.. On the 2d of June he sowed a few grains of wheat, one of the plants from which had thrown out so many sprouts, and from these so many stalks, that on the 18th of August he was enabled to divide it into eighteen parts, which he set out separately. By September and October these had so multiplied that he had set out sixty-seven stalks for the winter. With the first growth of the spring this multiplication and division went on till at the beginning of April the number of plants amounted to five hundred.

These plants proved more vigorous and productive than those under ordinary culture, so that the number of ears amounted to twenty-one thousand one hundred and nine; and they were remarkably fine, some containing from sixty to seventy grains each. The wheat, when separated from the straw, weighed forty-seven pounds and seven ounces, and measured within two quarts of a bushel, the estimated number of grains being five hundred and seventy-six thousand eight hundred and forty!

What wonderful forces, what subtle, expansive energy and growth, were silently sleeping in this small, dry, unpromising looking little seed. And how amazing the life that came from this single death. Who could have believed, without the actual sight, that the small and almost invisible germ wrapped in that one grain, could have multiplied and enlarged itself, and have diffused its vitalizing power through all these roots and shoots and stalks, into more than five hundred thousand other grains! How just the Saviour's words — "Except a corn of wheat fall into the ground and die, it abideth alone; but if it die, *it bringeth forth much fruit.*"

And how curious and admirable the constitution of this internal germ, the soul or spirit of the seed, that it should thus, under a change of circumstances seemingly so unfavorable as being buried in the earth, be able to incorporate into itself the impalpable, ethereal essence of light and air and moisture; that it should be able to assimilate them to its own nature, and so, according to the laws of its being, re-create itself, enlarge and diffuse its life almost indefinitely!

These are the facts on which the metaphor

of the apostle is founded; and the great truth taught by it is this: As certainly as the germ of the wheat is quickened into life, and larger life, by the death of the outer envelope or body, so certainly the soul is lifted into life, larger and more glorious life, by the dissolution of the mortal tabernacle in which it dwells while on earth. And the death of the body is as necessary to this renewal of the spirit, as the decomposition of the external integument or shell of the wheat-grain, is to the quickening of the germ.

And if this beautiful truth were received into the faith of the Christian, into the heart and life, the difference it would make in our living and dying, could not be expressed in words. It would clothe death with a new meaning, it would illuminate the realm of shadow as with the glory of the Lord, and transfigure all our thoughts and hopes of the future life.

This true, and Death gives a thousand-fold more than he takes away. Every earthly blessing left behind in going, is compensated for by a wealth of gifts showered upon the spirit on its arrival in the heavenly land. And though there may be pain and regret in parting with those who have loved us here, yet we are doubly comforted by thought of the glorious company of angels to which we go, and by the blessed knowledge that those we leave will by and by come to join us in the forward march from glory to glory!

It is something to be thankful for to have life on this earth, life with all its opportunities and gifts, with all its growths, and revelations of knowledge, and births and buildings up of character; but O how much more must it be in the great hereafter, when the unveiled splendors of the Lord's creation and the glories of his presence shall dawn upon the soul eager to try its newly-gotten liberty. Here the spirit is restrained and cramped and hindered by the encumbering flesh, its infirmities and wants and lusts; there it will be free, released from all its fetters, delivered from its long bondage to the earthly nature, from all conflict with weakness and temptation — free to grow, and unfold all its powers into new and diviner life; free to rise higher and higher in the scale of excellence; free to go upward from strength to strength, from beauty to beauty, from beatitude to beatitude, without limit and without hindrance.

No man can measure the life of the soul in the coming eternity, nor set a limit to its growth and expansion. No man can prophesy of the celestial glories which will dawn upon it from age to age along the track of that great future. But the spirit comes to all this only by the pathway that leads through the dark valley, and "over the river." Death alone strikes off its fetters, and opens the doors of its prison house, and brings it the freedom of new birth and larger growth. "It cannot be quickened except it die — but if it die, it bringeth forth much fruit." The old body perishes in order to give place to the new body — "there is a natural body and there is a spiritual body; howbeit that is not *first* which is spiritual, but that which is natural, and *afterward* that which is spiritual."

The first stage of the soul's existence is in the natural body, clothed upon with flesh; the second is in the spiritual body, clothed upon with the heavenly. The first is the infant state, the babyhood of our spiritual existence — is it desirable that it should never come to an end? especially when we remember what that little grain of wheat grew up to as soon as the fitting conditions were present? The babe may be very interesting and winning, but who would wish always to remain a babe? Why then wish the soul to continue always in its infancy, confined in this natural body, hungering, thirsting, weary, cramped in growth and activity? Is it not better that the natural body should give place to the spiritual body, that the outer investment of clay should die; that the inward germ of the spirit, like that of the wheat grain, may spring up into more abundant fruitfulness, under the genial influences of the heavenly latitudes?

The Death of the Body is really the Life of the Soul. It is the Spirit's second birth; and, through the Resurrection, its growth from infancy to manhood; the unfolding and amplification of all its latent powers, of all the hidden forces of its nature. The death of the natural body has released these from their fleshly imprisonment. And as the grain of corn, in contact with the fresh soil, swells, and bursts, and shoots up through the crumbling mould, first the blade, then the ear, after that the full corn in the ear; so the spirit, quickened by the warm and sunny breath of the celestial atmosphere, developes into new and vigorous growth, ripens into a wealth of fruitage, which it never could have attained to on earth.

Why, then, should we cling with such tenacity to the mortal body, the earthly life, the infant condition of the spirit? Why should we stand shivering at the thought of death, when, if Christians, we believe it opens out into this richer, grander life of freedom and immortality? this heavenly growth without impediment, or check, or limit?

When, therefore, the hour comes in which we must part from those who are dear to us, and pass on over the river which divides this from the Land of Promise: we may sorrow for the separation — it is human, it is natural, to weep in that hour — but let us be comforted in our grief for the death of the body, by our faith in the larger, nobler, the infinitely more glorious and blessed life of the spirit in the great Hereafter!

> Our life is onward, and our very dust
> Is longing for its change, that it may take
> New combinations; that the seed may break
> From its dark thraldom, where it lies in trust
> Of its great resurrection.
> And germs of beautiful vast thought, concealed
> Lie deep within the soul, which evermore
> Onward and upward strive. The last in place
> Enfolds the higher yet to be revealed,
> And each the sepulchre of that which went before.

V.

The Passage of the River, and the Preparation for it.

> Faith is the rainbow's form,
> Hung on the brow of heaven,
> The glory of the passing storm,
> The pledge of mercy given.
> It is the bright triumphal arch,
> Through which the saints to glory march.

HAVING thus far spoken of some of the peculiarly pleasing and suggestive figures under which the Scriptures represent Death, and its relations to the body and the spirit: it seems fitting, though allusion has been made to it in counselling the sick, that something more should be said of the spiritual preparation needful for this great event; of that faith, and religious experience, and Christian culture, which can alone render the passage of the river easy to us.

In order to realize in our own souls the divine power of the truths conveyed by these metaphors, and possess the courage and peace which they are designed to inspire in the hour of death, we must make a personal application of them, we must appropriate them as our own by faith, and a healthy religious experience.

It is not morality alone, not a good and just life merely, which makes the passage over the river easy, which takes the sting from death; but *faith*, faith in the facts symbolized by these scriptural metaphors, faith in God, faith in Christ as the Saviour who came to "deliver them who through fear of death were all their lifetime subject to bondage." In the hour of our departure there is no substitute for faith, there is nothing which can give us comfort and support but religion. In that hour it is not genius, nor talent, nor science, nor philosophy, but the Gospel only that is of any avail — the living words of Jesus who died and rose again, leading captivity captive, and giving unto men, as he ascended on high, the gifts of hope and faith and victory over Death.

As already remarked, we must make some effort in this direction. By a diligent and prayerful study of the Divine Word, we should seek to build our faith on a sure foundation; knowing *what* we believe, and *why* we believe, and therefore confident that we stand upon the Rock of ages. Thus diligent and earnest we shall, with the blessing of the Holy Spirit, attain to that knowledge of God and the Saviour which is life eternal in the soul of the believer. We shall realize that we are always in the hands of a kind Father, whether living or dying, in time or eternity. And satisfied of this, whenever our time shall come we shall be ready with the aged and pious Simeon to say, "Now Lord, lettest thou thy servant depart in peace, for mine eyes have seen thy salvation."

Blessed are they who have made this preparation of personal experimental religion; who have made God their refuge; for he is a very present help in time of trouble. Blessed are they who have sought, or are ready to seek, Christ as the Comforter, who is always ready to receive and bless those who seek him, even those coming at the eleventh hour. Sweet are the words of his invitation: "Come unto me all ye who labor and are heavy laden, and I will give you rest. Take my yoke upon you, and learn of me; for my yoke is easy, and my burden is light, and ye shall find rest unto your souls."

Blessed are they, thrice blessed, who, oppressed with sickness and suffering, and nigh unto the banks of the river of death, see Jesus as "the Way, the Life, and the Truth!" who rest in and rejoice in, that divine faith which sees God as the wise and merciful Ruler, the kind and tender Parent; which looks on life as a school for the trial and development of our moral and spiritual powers; which looks beyond the present into the future, and sees holiness and felicity and heaven as the final portion of the soul. This faith, accepted by the intellect and welcomed by the affections, gives to the departing soul a courage, a serenity, an absolute joy, the greatness of which to be understood must be experienced.

It has about it an actuality which only the dying one can know. It so takes hold on the realities of the spirit-world, its vision becomes so clear that the white-robed angels seem to sweep through the heavenly courts in visible procession; and the ear drinks in the sweet strains that float from the harps of the blessed, or breathe from the lips of adoring seraphim.

One example out of many will serve to illustrate the power and blessedness of this faith, and the wonderful manner in which it imparts strength to the spiritual vision, and becomes the evidence, or demonstration to the soul, of the actual existence of things not seen by the mortal eye. I refer to the death-scene of one who died as only the Christian can die.

She had embraced the gospel in the fulness of its salvation and its blessing, embraced it in her heart as well as mind. She lived by it, and in obedience to its precepts, and in the power of its faith. She honored it with a devotion — she loved it with an affection, which grew more and more ardent and absorbing up to the hour of her departure from earth to heaven. The fruit of this was a life of the highest happiness, and a death triumphant as the farewell of the saints of old.

Her sickness was short; and yet when assured that it must prove fatal, she exhibited perfect resignation to the will of God, and expressed a desire " to depart and be with Christ." Like Stephen of old, " full of faith and of the Holy Ghost," she looked beyond the waters, and " saw the heavens opened." Friends who could not sympathize in the fulness of her faith, but who loved her as a sister, stood near, anxiously watching to see her cross to the other side. Her husband, himself sceptical, laid his hand upon her forehead, and deeply impressed with the solemnities of that trying moment, addressed her, saying, "Dearest, *do* you believe that we shall meet again? — meet in heaven?" The spirit of faith, struggling for manifestation with an intensity which words could not utter, revealed itself in her countenance. "And all" that stood by, "looking steadfastly upon her, saw her face as it had been the face of an angel." "Believe!" said she, as she "looked up steadfastly unto heaven," "believe! *I know we shall meet again. I see it now!*"

And in this there was no excitement, no unnatural exaltation or rapture of the spirit. The summer evening is not calmer than was this dying saint; no hero of the highest sort was ever more perfectly self-possessed. It is easy to see, therefore, how such a faith realizes to itself the promises of God, and the revelations of the gospel. It seems to reach out and actually to lay hold on the coming joy, and to see, as with anointed eyes, the glorious mansions of the blessed, the house not made with hands, eternal in the heavens.

This humble and unknown woman saw what the wisest men on earth cannot see without faith. She was braver than the bravest, and richer than the richest, can ever be, without the wealth and the blessing of this faith, which smiles in the face of death; and while it puts one hand into his, puts the other into God's, and passes joyfully "over the river."

Plato, with his profound philosophy, and soaring speculations, and marvellous knowledge, cannot die as this Christian woman dies. She is profounder than he, and has a heavenly wisdom greater than anything written in the Divine Dialogues. But the death-scene of Socrates? It does not compare with this. *He hoped and submitted—she believed and triumphed!* He went forth into the dark, doubtful whither he went; she went forth confident, rejoicing, with the morning light of the resurrection breaking in upon her soul!

Look at La Place with his far-reaching science, disentangling the seemingly confused web of the spheres, thinking almost that he had his finger on the pulse of the universe; excluding God, by his material philosophy, from his own creation; wonderful as he is, vast as is the reach of his genius, he cannot die as this woman dies. All he knows he would give gladly, in the hour of death, for that simple, sublime, victorious faith, which sweeps majestic far above the stars, whose courses he so long and so painfully studied.

Can anything more be needed, then, than these sharp contrasts to show the infinite superiority of simple Christian faith over philosophy and science? over mere intellect, without the sanctification of faith and love?

Was not this humble disciple of Jesus, her heart full of the overflowing blessedness of the gospel, her eye kindling with the radiance of heaven, her soul lifting up its everlasting song of victory over death; just touching the grave as she went by, and then on white waving wing passing swiftly into the heavens to take her place among the angels — was she not greater than all these of whom we have spoken? And is there a more glorious triumph in all the earth than this?

If not, then, let us with all diligence strive for this living earnest faith, which looks through all the mists that float above the river of death, and, even while we are crossing, hears from afar the hallelujahs of the "seraphs that adore and burn."

> Yes, often in the hours of holy thought,
>   To the thirsting soul is given
> That power to pierce through the mist of sense,
>   To the beauteous scenes of heaven.
> Then very near seem its pearly gates,
>   And sweetly its harpings fall;
> Till the soul is restless to soar away,
>   And longs for the angel's call.
>
> I know when the silver cord is loosed,
>   When the veil is rent away,
> Not long and dark will the passage be
>   To the realms of endless day.
> The eye that shuts in the dying hour
>   Will open the next in bliss;
> The welcome will sound in the heavenly world,
>   Ere the farewell is hushed in this.

VI.

The World beyond the River, or the Glory of the Celestial.

>Since o'er thy footstool here below
>   Such radiant gems are strown,
> O what magnificence must glow,
>   Great God, around **thy** throne!
> So brilliant here these drops of light —
> There the full ocean rolls — how bright!

THE class of figures descriptive of death and the future life, which we have thus far brought to view, do not express all the phases of human desire and expectation. There is another element which often enters very largely into the thought of some; and to these activity, and not rest, activity, perpetual growth and progress to something higher and better, constitute the most attractive and delightful pictures of the spirit's life hereafter. And there are times, perhaps, when we are all open to the influence of this thought, and feel a longing to enter upon the career of knowledge and glory to which the vast and various creation of God invites us, and from which we are held back by these fetters of flesh and clay.

And, when we attempt to survey the measureless fields of the material universe, when we think of what this earth contains, and consider how small it is compared even with some of the other planets of our solar system; and when, going out of this system, we think of the suns and constellations which crowd the abysses of space, and reflect the splendors of divine wisdom and power — we cannot fail to realize, in some degree, the mighty influences operating on the soul to incite it to activity, and the multitudinous and glorious objects calling it on from wonder to wonder, from knowledge to knowledge.

And in view of this grand display of God's

creative power, it is impossible to feel that the future life is to introduce us to no nearer acquaintance with these far-off splendors. It is difficult to believe that when, liberated from the body, we are, for the first time, in a condition to visit and explore the distant constellations; and when the desire to behold and study the marvels and treasures of knowledge they contain grows upon us, and fills the soul with longings — that then we shall be compelled to forego this divine joy, to settle down into eternal quiet and inactivity in some corner of the universe, and call it heaven!

No, there is something better for us than this in the realization of the Christian idea of immortality. The starry skies which enfold us on all sides, are illuminated scrolls written all over by the hand of God with a kind of prophecy of the ever increasing acquisitions, the ever new discoveries, the intellectual growth and spiritual delight, which wait to welcome us when, escaped from these tabernacles of clay, we soar upward in the joyful freedom of the spirit.

And what thoughts crowd upon us when, from this stand-point we seek to map out to ourselves the vast regions of the soul's future life and enterprise; and to catalogue some of the numberless particulars which will engage its attention, and reward its inquiries. I look around upon this earth which makes the primary school of our life, where we learn our first lessons in the wonders of creation, and get our first experiences of intelligent beings — or, in a word, where we first come in contact with the mysteries of matter and of mind —

I look abroad upon the earth, and try to form some idea of it, to shape out some distinct impression of what it is, and what it holds. I see it is not one thing only, but many things. It is Europe, and Asia, and Africa, and America; France and England and Russia and the United States, and the islands of the sea; it is the Atlantic and the

Pacific, and lakes and rivers, and little brooks; it is hill and valley, the Andes and the prairies, and sand deserts, and dense forests, orchards and gardens and fields; it is mines of gold and silver, iron and lead and coal, and wells of oil; it is cities, and villages, and farm-houses everywhere; it is wild beasts and tame, and birds, and fishes, of every sort; it is a thousand millions of men and women and children, black and red and white, in their huts and palaces and homes; it is art and science, poetry, and music, and painting, and sculpture, philosophy and religion; it is being born, and living, and rejoicing, and sorrowing, and dying. This earth means all these things, and many thousands more. And what room for exploration and knowledge, what materials for study, what means for acquisition and growth. What endless variety of scene and subject for the active mind; and what infinite reward and blessing await the diligent and successful discoverer!

And when I have glanced thus over the

earth, which is all that is allotted us for this present life in the body — when I think, small as it is, how vast and innumerable its sources of instruction and enjoyment, how various and variable its objects of interest and delight — then I look up into the infinite depths, and gaze in silent wonder at the troops of worlds as they go by in glittering columns. I take up the telescope, and lo! whole hosts, unseen before, come marching into sight from the far-off spaces beyond the reach of the naked eye; great suns, as it were captains, with companies of stars following them, and shining constellations sweeping into the azure fields, till all the skies, as far as eye or instrument can reach, are filled with the gorgeous array!

Then I say to myself, What are these thronging hosts? *For* what are they? Why are they placed within reach of our vision, with all their bewildering beauty, if they are not for us? if we are never to visit them? But we never *can* visit them in this earthly body. *Then I am sure, for that very reason, that we shall visit them out of the body!* This is to be the work and the joy of the soul. Here is the sphere of its activity, the school of its future education, the temple of its worship; its heaven, in part, assuredly, in the coming eternity!

And what a sphere, what a broad and glorious theatre for action — these constellations and suns and moons, planets and earths, compared with some of which our little world is only as a boy's football or marble. And then all these worlds that we can see to the utmost boundaries of telescopic vision, are only the lamps lighting the entrance to the great temple of the Lord God, which still lies beyond, out of sight, infinite in extent, incomparable in its splendors.

And what was our brief definition of this earth, so various with its continents and seas, its exhibitions of nature and art, its wonders of life and intelligence! Consider then the treasures of knowledge and joy in these millions of worlds which will call to us, and beckon us on, through all eternity! What ever shifting exhibitions of natural scenery — what new fields for science, for study and contemplation — what new forms of being, and new orders of intelligences, and ever-rising ranks of spiritual life! O what a glorious future this is to go to! What an exultant life for the soul, when Death strikes off the fetters of the flesh, and sets it free; when dust returns to dust whence it came, and the spirit returns to God who gave it! What if the path to this do lead down for a little into the dark, cannot we tread it firmly and fearlessly, when we know that it leads up finally into the eternal splendors?

> The soul of man was made to walk the skies;
> Delightful outlet of her prison here!
> And, disencumbered from her chains, the ties
> Of toys terrestrial, there she roves at large;
> In full proportion lets loose all her powers;
> And wonderful herself, through wonder strays;
> Grows conscious of her birth celestial; breathes
> More life, more vigor, in her native air,
> And feels herself at home among the stars!

VII.

Employments of the Future Life.

> O Father! all sufficient! over all!
> Enrich me with the knowledge of thy works —
> Lift me to heaven; thy rolling wonders there,
> World beyond world, in infinite extent,
> Profusely scattered o'er the blue immense,
> Show me; their motions, periods and their laws.

THE Scriptures do not enter into details in regard to the future life; but deal mostly in the broad declaration that we shall be as angels in the resurrection world, immortal, holy and happy. Still, there are some allusions and indirect references to the employments of the heavenly state, and some inferences legitimately deducible from existing facts and arrangements in the providence of God, confirmatory of the preceding argument; and which seem to unfold to us the divine plan of blessedness in the future life, or at least to indicate something of its various activity. Occasionally we have glimpses of light which open upon a diversified disposition of affairs in the spirit world, and an endless variety of blissful employments, adapted to the different capacities, or degrees of developement of human souls.

And this very difference in capacity or spiritual power, as well as in the degree of advancement, seems to require a corresponding variety of action, and diversity in the kinds of happiness. Unless all remain at the same point of spiritual growth at which they enter on the future life; unless all souls are, as it were, run in the same mould, and endowed with exactly the same measure of strength, the same emotions, and desires, and thoughts — there must be a great variety both in the kinds of happiness and in the degrees. And why not? Is heaven less fertile in resources for the employment and enjoyment of its inhabitants, than earth?

How various the sources of enjoyment and of pleasurable activity in the present. How manifold and dissimilar the methods adopted in securing happiness. And is it not probable — nay, certain that the future life will furnish as much room for action and developement of character; furnish as various employment for the intellect, as numerous sources of gratification, as the present life? It is not easy, as before remarked, for the thoughtful Christian to believe that our only employment, the only source of happiness for the soul hereafter, will be in singing songs of praise, or in formal ascriptions of glory and honor to God and the Lamb. It is not accordant with the arrangements of divine providence and government so far as we have any knowledge of them. It is not in harmony with the intellectual nature of man, which requires, as indispensable to its highest enjoyment, activity, continued movement and advancement, ceaseless additions to its materials for thought and study, and a constant enlargement of its sphere of operations.

The soul will be glad and grateful for the past; but it will require that the present and the future shall not compel it to idleness, to the mere passive enjoyment of dreaming of the past. It will ask for the new blessedness of ever fresh exhibitions of the power and wisdom and beneficence of the Infinite; for continued discoveries, and the joy of ever-increasing knowledge and spiritual power. And if this be not provided for in some way, it would seem as if the mere change of worlds cannot make heaven for it. There must be an adaptation of condition and circumstances to the nature of the soul, to the elements of its life, to realize the true idea of heaven.

It were well to form our opinions on this point from those passages which repeat to us the songs and ascriptions of praise to God, from angels and cherubim, and those exalted spirits that bow before the throne, saying,

"Holy, holy Lord God Almighty — Glory be to thee in the highest, and honor and power; for thou hast made all things — great and marvellous are thy works; just and true are thy ways. The heavens shall declare thy wonders; all thy works shall praise thee, and thy saints shall bless thee!" These hymns of praise show their source in a knowledge of the glorious works of God, in admiration of the stupendous exhibitions of divine power, wisdom and goodness in the illimitable fields of creation.

We may imagine, and not without great probability, that these blessed, angelic beings, after extended excursions to some distant province or portion of the boundless empire of the Almighty — after having surveyed some remote system of worlds, and made themselves familiar with their various aspects; the details of their physical history; the changes of surface; the stages of geological developement; the distribution of animal and vegetable life; the character, development, organism, moral relations and mental endowments of the intelligent inhabitants of each — after beholding these multiplied exhibitions of the divine energy, skill and benevolence, — we may well imagine them returning from this delightful and instructive excursion, and gathering about the throne of the Ancient of Days, with these ascriptions of glory and honor, as the utterance of joy, of adoration and gratitude for what they have seen and learned on this, to them, new theatre of the divine operations.

And in view of some such event as this, how much more force and meaning are given to the Revelator's language, when he says that, overwhelmed, as it were, with the sense of God's infinite power and wisdom, and with the extent and splendor of his creation, they fell down and "worshipped Him that liveth forever and ever; and cast their crowns before the throne, saying, Thou art worthy, O Lord! to receive glory and honor and power: for thou hast created all things, and for thy pleasure they are and were created."

And then consider for a moment the extent of the field open to the glorified spirit. No language is adequate to the grandeur of the theme. The number of systems within reach of our telescopes is reckoned at nearly eighty millions. Sir William Herschell informs us that, in surveying a portion only of the milky way, one of the nebulæ visible from our planet, there passed, in the space of seven minutes, fifty thousand stars across the field of his telescope! Suppose each one of these suns to have in revolution about it some thirty planetary bodies, primary and secondary, and we have in one portion of the universe within range of our instruments a congregation of, 2,400,000,000 of worlds! And then, let us add to this the fact that the nearest of these suns is, at least, twenty billions of miles distant from us — and if we have no very definite conception of these vast numbers and spaces, as we probably have not; we are certainly very powerfully impressed with the immensity of the creation, and of the field of investigation opened to the soul hereafter. And consider that all this is but the threshold of the temple of nature — that all these suns and stars visible to us, are, as one has singularly said, only the "street-lamps of the city of God."

And then, when we have glanced at the extent of this field of action and enjoyment, imagine, if possible, the infinite variety it affords for inquiry and intellectual and moral entertainment. How many questions crowd upon the mind for consideration. "Are all these vast globes inhabited? If so, what is their history in the past and the present? Are the inhabitants pure moral intelligences, or are they exposed to the inroads of physical and moral evil? What are the gradations of rank and intellect among them? What sciences do they cultivate? What knowledge have they of other portions of the divine empire? What discoveries have they made of the perfections of the Deity, of the plan of his government, and the extent of his dominions?"

What corporeal vehicles do they employ in connection with the material world? What kind of organization are they endowed with? In what organs of sense or faculties of mind do they differ from man? What is their social condition? What means of improvement and progress have they? What is the physical character of the planet they inhabit? What diversity of external scenery greets their sight? What celestial glories are hung out for their contemplation in the canopy of heaven? What visible displays of the power and wisdom of God in his works are presented to them? What exhibitions of his goodness in nature or by revelation have they been favored with? These and a thousand other inquiries rise up before the mind in this world; but we have no answer. What variety of employment and happiness, then, will the soul find hereafter in searching into these things, and increasing its knowledge of the wondrous works and ways of the Infinite One; and, through this, lifting itself into ever-growing adoration and love. And when we remember that this is only one department of inquiry, and yet so abundant in its contributions to the active enjoyments of heavenly spirits; how vast and innumerable must be the sources which God has supplied for the improvement, instruction and blessedness of the soul in the future life!

It is certainly strange that, to so great an extent, Christians should have regarded the almost sole employment of the redeemed to be, the celebration in songs and hallelujahs of the grace of God in the redemption through Christ — and this throughout the ceaseless ages of eternity; while the boundless and infinitely glorious universe of God, with its numberless suns and systems, with its magnificent displays of the divine perfections, lies all around them unvisited, unknown and uncared for; while poetry, with which creation is rife, philosophy, science, history, and the activity and the joy of learning and instructing, are all neglected and forgotten!

Doubtless the first will constitute an important part of the beatitudes of the heavenly life; but surely the last will contribute largely to the same result. Certainly every well instructed Christian will confess that the views we have presented seem much more accordant with the character of God, the nature of the human soul, and what we may reasonably suppose to be the object of its future endless life — viz: advancement forever in spiritual blessedness, which is itself the product of growth forever in the knowledge of the Divine Being, his government, perfections and infinite beneficence, whether revealed in Christ or in his works.

And with the various capacities, and the different stages of developement of spiritual beings, what room for mutual aid, instruction and enjoyment. Continually arriving from the innumerable worlds which people the vast regions of the universe; will not these new comers require the guidance and teaching of those that have been longer inhabitants of the celestial sphere, and made farther progress in heavenly culture and education? and will not both, teacher and taught, find a common joy in the employment? Who that ever looked upon an affectionate parent instructing his child, pointing out the beauties of a flower or a plant, or the glories of the starry host, or recounting some history, or entertaining legend — who, beholding this, and witnessing the calm joy and satisfaction beaming from the face of the parent, and the intense interest and delight that danced in the eye, and lighted up the glowing countenance of the young learner, did not feel that both alike were blessed? did not feel that of all scenes our life exhibits, this is among the most lovely; the most perfect picture of mutual tenderness and mutual joy?

And why should the heavenly life be robbed of it? Why may not the more advanced and exalted spirits so take the direction and instruction of the younger; and lead them forth from world to world, and initiate them into the mysteries, and unfold to them the splendors of the divine workmanship? Why not take them in charge as they enter the celestial sphere, and in familiar instructive converse walk with them through the sounding aisles, and along the lofty galleries of Nature's great cathedral; till they shall come at last, filled with wonder and joy, to the chancel, the sanctuary, the Holy of holies, — where God the Infinite manifests himself in glory ineffable: where cherubim and seraphim, in turn, continually do cry, Holy, Holy Lord God Almighty — great and marvellous are thy works! glorious in wisdom and power art Thou, doing wonders continually — Blessed be thy name, Thou King of kings, and Lord of lords!

> O sometimes, when adown the sky,
>   The fiery sunset lingers,
> Heaven's golden gates swing inward noiselessly,
>   Unlocked by unseen fingers, —
>
> And while they stand a moment half ajar,
>   Gleams from the inner glory,
> Stream brightly through the azure vault afar,
>   And half reveal the story.

VIII.

The Attractions of Heaven.

> Nor bard, nor sage may comprehend
> The heaven of love to which we tend,
> Our home is not this mortal clime;
> Our life hath not its bounds in time;
> And death is but the cloud that lies
> Between our souls and Paradise!

BUT there are other elements of our nature beside the intellectual, which find their employment and joy in the world of light and glory. We have already alluded to this point, but it has so much comfort in it that we shall enlarge upon it, even at the risk of seeming to repeat some things already said. Not only the mind, but the heart also, the religious and social affections, will find attractions there. "In the Father's house there are many mansions," and in each one of them we shall find some new delight, some dear remembered face, some precious jewel treasured on earth, some beautiful and beloved spirit who ministered to our comfort and happiness while we were pilgrims in this lower world, afar from home. Surely we shall not be alone there — a father or mother will meet us; a husband or wife or beloved child, a brother or sister, or some dear friend will welcome us.

Yes, one of the most grateful and pleasing thoughts of the future life is that which renews the loving and tender associations of this. Heaven will be to the future, what home is to the present life; the sacred place where the affections may utter themselves without restraint, where the heart may gather up its treasures, rejoicing in its everlasting heritage of love and blessedness. There our cherished and idolized ones will gather around us, and fold their arms about us, and engage in sweet and pleasant converse. They who walked with us in the cheerful sunlight, and in the solemn shadows, of our earthly life. They who bore with us the heat and burthen of the day. They who loved us as we yearned to be loved, and on whom the gushing tenderness of the heart was poured out like summer rain upon the fields. They whose sweet faces were like smiles from heaven on our earthly sorrow, and whose kind words fell on the worn heart like dew on withering plants,—

> "They the young and strong, who cherished
>   Noble longings for the strife,
> By the roadside fell and perished,
>   Weary with the march of life —
> They, the holy ones and weakly
>   Who the cross of suffering bore,
> Folded their pale hands so meekly,
>   Spake with us on earth no more."

All these shall come to us again — and O how blessed the meeting — "a family in heaven, no wanderer lost." We shall live again — we shall be together again. Love is immortal as the soul. And the poorest and most hopeless of earth's children, the most darkened and wayward and forsaken, is still loved of some one in the great crowd of life — *and God loves us all!*

Yes, we shall meet again, all of us, and rejoice together in the glorious light of the Sun of Righteousness. If it were not so, the gift of a future life would be of little worth. Take from us those we love, and you take away all that makes Heaven desirable.

> For " O how dark, how drear, how lone
> Would seem the brightest world of bliss,
> If wandering through each radiant sphere,
> We failed to meet the loved of this."

Tell me that I am never again to behold the precious ones who have cared for me and watched over me here, whose spirits were toned in chord with mine, whose gentle ministries of affection have given life all its beauty and blessedness — tell me I shall never see nor be with these again, and I cannot go in peace, I will not say to the grave — but not even to a life, however glorious, where they are not. No; and I say it not hastily, but with much thought — I could not desire a heaven, where I am not to find those dear beings who have woven themselves like golden threads into the very texture of my soul, and have become to me as the pulse of my heart.

Thanks be to God the Father, and to our Lord Jesus Christ, I *shall* find them — every one of them in some of the many mansions of the Father's house; and there together we shall lift up the hymn of redemption, and behold the glory of the Lord's creation, and worship in the beauty of holiness; for there we shall be renewed in the spirit, and in a higher and holier sense we shall be the children of God, being children of the Resurrection!

There is, then, everything in heaven to make it attractive, everything to call our thoughts thitherward. *There* is light and truth without darkness or error; *there* knowledge is increasing without hindrance, and happiness without limit; *there* are the lost, and loved, and beautiful of earth; *there* is a reunion of all the broken links and sundered ties of affection; *there* is rest and peace, for "God shall wipe away all tears from their eyes; and there shall be no more death, neither sorrow, nor crying, neither shall there be any more pain, for the former things are passed away." In the words of one, to whom all this has now become a reality: "Why should I fear to die? Let me rather welcome death as the beautiful gate that leads to such a blessed immortality.

Immortal life! my heavenly home! How many attractions it has! how many loved objects I shall meet there! how many dear and precious memories will be revived there!

I shall see and know my heavenly Father there as I have never seen or known him on this earth. How kind and gracious he has been to me! how precious are all his promises! How sweet then is the thought, I shall see him unveiled in all his glory, and know him as my best and truest friend!

I shall see Jesus, my Saviour; he who

loved me and died for me. How many reasons are there for loving him more than my poor, sinful heart has ever done! But I shall see him in my heavenly home, and know him as mine and the world's Saviour.

I shall see and recognize all those dear ones of my heart, who have passed away into the spirit-world. Their presence, their kindly spirit and affection, their genial friendship and love, made this world very bright and beautiful, but now they have left it. Welcome, then, thrice welcome the kind hand that shall guide me to those I love. Dear ones will be left behind; for them must still be the toil and struggle and disappointment; for them the bitterness of parting; but for me, oh, how blessed will be that reunion!"

And there is yet another pleasing thought, not alluded to in this extract, which gives attractiveness to the heavenly life — we shall meet the great and wise and good of all times and nations, and mingle in their society, and rejoice in their fellowship. There we shall see and commune with **Moses and Isaiah**, with **Paul and John**; with **Confucius and Socrates, and Plato, and Origen**; with **Fenelon, and Howard, and Channing**; with **Bacon and Newton, and** a host of others, who, by the splendor of their intellects, or by the saintly goodness of their lives, glorified the earth, and are now themselves glorified in heaven. What delight to speak with such as these, to listen to their instructive speech, **to hear them** recount their intellectual triumphs, their visions of the glory of the Lord **Creator as displayed in his works, their deeds of Christian benefaction, their** divinely beautiful spiritual experiences, their great deliverance from their earthly bondage, and their visits, since **they were clothed upon** with bodies celestial, to the clustered worlds and constellated wonders **that flame** along the far-off abysses **of the universe!** O what a joy awaits **us in such society** as this; **and how it draws the soul toward the heavenly land,** where **only it is possible to behold and speak with these** glorified **spirits.**

And though we do not love the elect and precious of earth any less, yet it takes something from the bitterness of death, when we think of the great company of noble minds whom we go to join. And we are doubly comforted in the thought that, by and by, those whom we leave behind will come to us, and share with us in all the delights of this heavenly intercourse with the wise and the noble, the great and the good, of all ages and generations!

Oh yes, we *shall* meet in a world that is bright,
Where God and the Lamb are the glory and light,
Where sorrow is ended, and tears are all dried,
And the love of the faithful no longer is tried.

O ye who have tasted affliction's strong power,
Remember who governs the desolate hour,
And with faith's steady vision keep strong on your way,
Assured that your strength shall be still as your day.

Thus every dear spirit whose conflict is past,
Hath labored and striven in faith to the last;
And if we are faithful, as they whom we love,
" Tho' we miss them below, we shall meet them above."

IX.

Attractions of Earth.

O yes, I love the earth — its cares and sorrows,
　Its bounding hopes, its feelings fresh and warm,
Each cloud it wears, and every light it borrows,
　Loves, wishes, fears, the sunshine and the storm —
I love them all; but closer still the loving
　Twine with my being's chords, and make my life.

BUT after all that may be said of the glories of the future, and of the attractions of heaven, earth also has its attractions, which it is hard to go away from and leave — sweet pictures from nature, pleasant homes, delightful memories of the past, bright hopes of the future, extensive usefulness, a well earned reputation; and, above all, dear friends and companions, fond and faithful parents, a devoted husband, an affectionate wife, beloved children, who, by their constant kindness and watchful tenderness, have made all the years of our life beautiful and blessed. These are some of the attractions which make life on earth desirable, some of the strong ties which hold us to the present, and the sundering of which give to death much of its bitterness. It is hard to die, and leave all these. It is hard to die, when there is so much to live for. If we could all go together, it would be less difficult; it would be easy to die, and go home in one company to the Father's house.

Certainly there is truth in all this; and it would be equally wrong and useless to ignore it, or to pretend that it ought not to have any weight with a Christian. It is our common human nature which speaks in this; it is the heart pleading for its treasures with a sacred constancy, with a voice of tenderness, which the most devout and submissive Christian cannot, and would not wish, to silence. In loving the Saviour, we do not cease to love our friends; nor is the highest trust in God inconsistent with the fondest attachments of human affection. And the ever compassionate Father does not ask us, in remembering and confiding in Him, to forget, or cease to cling to, those who have lovingly nestled down in the secret places of our hearts.

Still, it is only just and right that we should have a reasonable confidence in God, that we should believe in the wise beneficence of his dealings with us, even if they do disappoint our wishes; and we, in our blindness, cannot see the good they are designed to work out for us. This assuredly the Father has a right to ask at our hands in return for the many thousand proofs of his goodness to us in the past; as well as because of the numerous positive declarations and precious promises of his holy word, that in all he does with us, for us, to us, he is steadily seeking our highest interests and happiness. We see through a glass darkly now, and know only in part; and we must not expect, therefore, to see as God sees, or perfectly to understand his thoughts or his ways, which are higher than ours as the heavens are higher than the earth.

You, my friend, in the midst of your life and usefulness, held by so many strong cords of affection, feel that it is very hard to die; and you cannot see how your death can have any good in it for yourself, or for those dear ones who so fondly cling to you, and shelter themselves so trustingly under the protection of your love. I will not pretend that I clearly see it either; but I know that there is much good hidden in evil that I did not see once, which is now distinctly visible to me; and events, which, at the time, I deplored as the greatest sorrows of my life, have long ago shaped themselves into the greatest blessings. And so I have learned to be slow and humble in my judgment of the ways of God; and I try, however great the struggle it costs, to pray in my sorrows, as well as in my joys, living or dying: "*Thy* will, and not mine, be done."

And have not you, my dear friend, required from *your* children the same confidence and loving submission which you so reluctantly yield toward your Father in heaven? How often have the plans, which your judgment and affection devised for the good of your boy, the pride of your heart, conflicted with his wishes and desires. He had his own views of the best method of securing happiness; and perhaps believed that freedom from all restraint, the society of his mates, the absence of all study and work, and a perpetual round of amusements, made up the sum of human enjoyment. On the other hand, you *knew* that education and knowledge, employment, usefulness and a manly tone of thought and character, were the surest and only path to happiness.

And this is exactly the relation existing between God the Father and you his child. To your boy play seems better than school, but it is not; and when boyhood passes into manhood he will see his mistake, and thank you for denying his prayers and preferences. And yet it is a real grief to him to give up his games and frolics; but it is a blessed grief, for it brings him to knowledge and honor and true happiness. In reality his grief is joy in disguise.

Is it not so with you, with us all, when our will does not agree with the will of God, when our plans do not harmonize with his? You wish to live, to stay in this world with those whose love and companionship are so dear to you — this is a greater good to you than to depart and be here no more. In a word, life is the only good, death is the only evil. But it is plain that God thinks differently, or he would not now be leading you down to the banks of the river of death. And are you not safer in trusting to his knowledge than to your own? are you surer of abiding blessedness for yourself or your beloved ones, when you follow the path of your own wishes, instead of the path of his wisdom?

In a word, to come directly to the real issue, if your Father in heaven should speak to you audibly, and tell you, that of his infinite knowledge he had determined it was better for you to die now, would you be willing, if it were left to you, to take the risk of living? Would you dare the solemn responsibility of setting up your decision against his? Now this is really the state of the case. God *has* spoken to you, not audibly, but by the fact of your present condition, and told you that it is better for you to go hence over the river, into the realms of immortal life! Had you not then better leave it with Him, your Father in heaven, whose wisdom never errs, and whose love will never fail you? and will you not try, with a sweet and childlike trust, to say, even if the tears come with it: "Thy will, O God, and not mine, be done." Be sure that, with effort and prayer, strength will come, and resignation, and by and by, peace passing knowledge and expression. And it will be fulfilled unto you at last, the promise of Jesus to his disciples: "I will pray the Father, and he shall send the Comforter in my name, that he may abide with you forever, even the Spirit of Truth."

"At last"— for this perfect calm and resignation will not come at once, and, as remarked, not without effort. No one, however firm his faith, ever met a great trial, or bore a great sorrow, with patience and a cheerful submission, without first passing through a season of self-conflict. Even the Saviour had this experience, and it is this very fact that makes him nearer and dearer to every weary and suffering soul. It is a thought full of comfort that we have an "high-priest who can be touched with the feeling of our infirmities;" for in that he himself hath suffered, he is able to succor all them that come unto him. And consider how Jesus was in the very bosom of God and knew his counsels, and knew the saving purpose of his own death, and the glorious resurrection which was to follow; and yet, when the hour of trial came, how great was that agony in the garden! Yes, even Christ struggled with his lot, and exclaimed, "O Father, if it be possible, let this cup pass from me!" and it was not till *after* this struggle and sorrowful exclamation, that the spirit rose triumphant over the quivering nerves and fainting pulses of the flesh, and uttered itself in the divine prayer: "Nevertheless, not as I will, but as thou wilt."

If this, then, was the experience of our blessed Lord, surely you must not expect, frail and feeble as you are, to conquer yourself, and sunder all the ties that bind you to life, in a moment, and without any inward conflict. No, it will require time and effort, and much thought and prayer, and communion with your own soul and with the Holy Spirit. And you should not accuse your faith or piety because it is so. God knows your heart, and looks upon you with compassion and tender pity, and will help you to overcome at last. He does not say to you "sorrow not"— but "sorrow not as those who are without hope." He asks you to trust in him as a refuge and support, and to receive into your heart the great hope of the gospel, the hope of immortal life, which he has given as a comfort and an encouragement in the hour of trial. He calls upon you to appropriate to yourself the blessed promises of his word, that "none of us liveth to himself, and no man dieth to himself, for whether we live, we live unto the Lord; and whether we die, we die unto the Lord: whether we live therefore, or die, we are the Lord's." "For to this end Christ both died, and rose, and revived, that he might be Lord both of the dead and the living." And "we know that if our earthly house of this tabernacle were dissolved, we have a building of God, a house not made with hands, eternal in the heavens."

And in parting with your loved ones, his Word of truth reminds you that the separation is only for a little time. The difference is not that you die, and they live; but that you die to-day, and they die to-morrow. It is a difference of time only, and not of fact or condition. The same experience awaits us all. Life is short at the longest, only an handbreadth; and then those you leave behind come to join you, and you will be together forevermore. And till then he has promised to watch over them, and keep them, and cause all things to work together for their good! Leave them, then, in his hands, for he will care for them, and not a hair of their heads shall fall to the ground without his permission. And it may be that, when you have crossed over to the other shore, he will still permit you to behold them with open vision, to follow them in all their earthly paths, to witness their joys, and to understand the beneficent meaning and use of all their sorrows. The river of death is very narrow, and though with our dim earthly eyes we are not able to discover those on the other side; it is possible that they, with their clear spiritual sight, may easily look over to this side. Whether it be so or not, go forth cheerfully trusting in God, and surrendering all your earthly treasures into his care, whether husband or wife, parents or children. Go, confident that you and yours are the objects of his parental regard, of his everlasting love.

If life could be always alluring and bright
As it seems in its innocent morning,
No shade on its prospect — sweet visions at night
The calm of its slumber adorning —
Too fondly and closely our spirits would trust
In the pleasures which earth seemed to give them,
And slowly and faintly would rise from the dust
As if it were sorrow to leave them.

'Tis well that some shadows flit over our way,
Some clouds hover darkly above it,
They teach us while Earth is a scene of decay,
It were folly too deeply to love it;
Its joys and its hopes, for a moment which gleam,
Soon fade like a vision at even,
While our spirits turn gladly from Earth's passing dream
To the glorious sunlight of Heaven.

X.

The Dying do not Suffer.

> Lift up thy drooping head,
> Thou who in gloom and dread
>   Hast lain so long;
> And raise thy hands and pray,
> And God will smooth thy way,
>   And make thee strong.

ONE fact more demands attention before closing this portion of our work. Many persons, excellent in character, Christian in faith, have an unconquerable dread of dying — not of being dead, not of anything that may come after they are dead — but of the supposed agony of dying. It is a very common belief that there is dreadful suffering, inexpressible bodily anguish, attendant upon the process of death, or the dissolution of the connection between the soul and the body.

But mostly this is an entire mistake. A brain fever, the inflammatory rheumatism, a single day's endurance of severe neuralgia, has more torture in it than twenty deaths. As a rule death itself, as far as we have any data for a conclusion, is accompanied with comparatively little or no pain, or physical suffering. And this for a very simple reason, where there is lengthened sickness, or acute disease, viz: the power of suffering is exhausted before it comes to death; the nervous system is completely prostrated, and the muscles relaxed; and thus sensation is gradually deadened, pain ceases, consciousness slowly fades out, and the dying one is as if he were falling into a profound and quiet sleep. This is the prevailing witness of those who have gone down to the very gates of death, and returned again; even in those cases where consciousness was perfect, and everything within the room was seen and heard and understood, without the power of expression in word or motion.

The truth is, the pain is in the disease, not in death, and all the agony and suffering are over before the final moment of departure; and there is not only an absence of pain in death itself or in dying, but often the sweetest quiet, a blessed sense of relief and repose, and sometimes the most beautiful visions of coming light and glory.

Touching this subject, the following, from high authority, will be found comforting and instructive:

"The pain of dying must be distinguished from the pain of the previous disease; for when life ebbs, sensibility declines. As death is the final extinction of corporeal feelings, so numbness increases as death comes on. The prostration of disease, like healthful fatigue, engenders a growing stupor — a sensation of subsiding softly into a coveted repose. The so-called agony can never be more formidable than when the brain is the last to go, and the mind preserves to the end a rational cognizance of the state of the body. Yet persons thus situated commonly attest that there are few things in life less painful than the close. 'If I had strength enough to hold a pen,' said William Hunter, 'I would write how easy and delightful it is to die.' 'If this is dying,' said the niece of Newton, 'it is a pleasant thing to die;' 'the very expression,' adds her uncle, 'which another friend of mine made use of on her death-bed a few years ago.' The same words have so often been uttered under similar circumstances, that we could fill pages with instances which are only varied by the name of the speaker. 'If this be dying,' said Lady Clenorchy, 'it is the easiest thing imaginable.' 'I thought that dying had been more difficult,' said Louis XIV. 'I did not suppose it was so sweet to die,' said Francis Suarez, the Spanish theologian. An agreeable surprise was the prevailing sentiment with them all. They expected the stream to terminate in the dash of the torrent, and they found it was losing itself in the gentlest current. The whole of the faculties seem sometimes concentrated on the placid enjoyment. The day Arthur Murphy died he kept repeating from Pope:

> ' Taught half by reason, half by mere decay,
> To welcome death, and calmly pass away.'

"A second and common condition of the dying is to be lost to themselves and all around them, in utter unconsciousness. Countenance and gestures might in many cases suggest that, however dead to the external world, an interior sensibility still remained. But we have the evidence of those whom disease has left at the eleventh hour, that while their supposed sufferings were pitied by their friends, existence was a blank. The delirium of fever is distressing to witness; but the victim awakes from it as from a heavy sleep, totally ignorant that he has passed days and nights tossing wearily and talking wildly."

And what, let me add, can be more distressing to look upon than the distorted features and violent spasms which attend epileptic fits? Yet it is well known that there is no suffering in these cases; those affected being often wholly unconscious even of the attack, though uttering the most dismal groans, and seeming to be in greatest agony. So what we sometimes witness when standing by the bedside of the dying; the convulsion of the limbs, the painful expression of the features, and other signs of suffering, are, as a rule, purely muscular, without any more pain than attends epileptic affections, or the sudden contraction and jumping of the muscles which frequently precedes falling asleep. And those who have recovered from this seemingly dying condition, which includes all there is in physical death, declare that, all suffering ceased before they reached this point, and that they were nearly unconscious, or in a state of perfect quiet.

These testimonies of the dying might be increased to any extent, showing that, as a rule, whatever perturbations may have preceded, there is in the article of death itself an almost entire absence both of physical and mental suffering. Heaven seems very merciful to us in the last hour, and, soothing all our pains, vouchsafes to us a quiet and peaceful departure to the land of rest. Dr. Black, worn out by age, and a tendency to pulmonary hemorrhage, which obliged him to live very low, while eating his customary frugal meal, fell asleep, and died in so tranquil a manner, that he did not spill the contents of the spoon which he held in his hand. And the death of Sir Charles Blagden was in much the same way; for while enjoying a social meal with some of his intimate friends, he died in his chair so quietly that not a drop of the coffee in the cup, which he held in his hand, was spilled. Haller died feeling his pulse, and when it was almost gone, he turned to his brother physician, and said cheerfully, "My friend, the artery ceases to beat," and quietly breathed his last. Petrarch and Leibnitz both died, the hand still holding the book they were reading; and Lucan, Roscommon and

Klopstock died repeating their own poetry. Schiller, when dying, replied to an inquiring friend, "I am feeling calmer and calmer." And the poet Keats, on being asked how he felt, just before he died, answered with characteristic sweetness and beauty, "Better, my friend; I feel the daisies growing over me."

When Mozart had given the finishing touches to that wonderful "*Requiem*," his last and sweetest composition, he fell into a quiet and composed slumber. On awaking, he said to his daughter, "Come hither, my Emilie, my task is done; the Requiem — *my* Requiem is finished." "O no," said the gentle girl, the tears filling her eyes, "you will be better now; and let me go and bring you something refreshing." "Do not deceive yourself, my love," he replied, "I am beyond human aid; I am dying, and I look to Heaven's mercy only for aid. You spoke of refreshment — take these last notes of mine; sit down by my piano here — sing them with the hymn of your sainted mother — let me once more hear those tones which have so long been my solace and delight." His daughter complied, and, with a voice tremulous with emotion, sung the following :

> Spirit! thy labor is o'er!
> The race of the mortal is run;
> Thy steps are now bound for the untrodden shore,
> And the race of immortals begun.
>
> Spirit! look not on the strife
> Or the pleasures of earth with regret —
> Pause not on the threshold of limitless life,
> To mourn for the day that is set.
>
> Spirit! no fetters can bind,
> No wicked have power to molest;
> There the weary, like thee, and the wretched, shall find
> A home, and a mansion of rest.
>
> Spirit! how bright is the road
> For which thou art now on the wing!
> Thy home it will be with thy Saviour and God,
> Their praises forever to sing.

As the last notes died away into silence, the spirit of the great composer took its flight heavenward; and as the daughter turned for the accustomed words of approval, she saw only the sweet smile of contentment which still lingered on the face of death; and revealed the unutterable peace of his dying.

The departure of *Beethoven*, whose musical compositions are still the delight of mankind, was equally beautiful and impressive. He was entirely deaf, and never knew the joy of hearing his own wonderful creations. He had been for some time slowly sinking away into the arms of death, when one day he suddenly revived; and, as a bright smile lighted up his expressive features, he softly murmured, "*I shall hear in heaven!*" and immediately he began singing in a low, but clear and distinct voice, one of his own beautiful hymns — and so passed "over the river" into the land of immortal song, and joined the choir of angels.

These examples, gathered from all conditions of life and culture, have been multiplied for the purpose of comforting those who are approaching death, and imparting courage to those who dread the physical suffering supposed to accompany dying. They show that the rule is the reverse of what most persons think it; and that the facts, as far as we have them, prove that the suffering, as we have already said, is not in death, but in the sickness which precedes it; that dying is very like falling into a quiet sleep.

And there is mostly also an absence not only of bodily distress, but of mental distress. The fear of death, and the struggle against it, and all unreconciliation, seem to fade away as death itself approaches, and leave us calm and placid as a summer evening. It is certainly very remarkable, this almost universal experience. Sir James Brodie, as the result of his extensive practice and long observation, not only decides that the act of dying is seldom in any sense a painful process; but also declares that he has "never known but two instances in which, in the act of dying, there were manifest indications of the fear of death."

A similar witness is given by a well-known lady connected with the Western Sanitary

Commission, who has been present at many hundreds of death-scenes among the soldiers. In only two cases out of the multitude coming under her observation, was there any manifest terror, or mental disturbance, at the approach of death.

In confirmation of these testimonies the writer of this book can add the experience and observation of a pastoral ministry of more than thirty years. In very few instances out of hundreds dying in youth, and in old age, and in the full flush of meridian life, has there been any *appearance* even of great physical suffering; and he cannot recall a single example of unconquerable terror in the act of dying. On the contrary, though in many cases there has been a fear of death during sickness, a dread of dying, yet when the hour came, it had all passed away, and in the place of it there was a perfect resignation, and a peace passing expression.

And further illustration of this interesting fact might be given, if one who has been down to the gates of death and returned again, might speak of his own personal experience. But there is something sacred beyond speech in the memories of that solemn and holy time, in that sense of God's nearness, in that profound calm and serenity of soul, the absence of all disturbing influences both of body and of mind, of all regret and earthly longings; the blessed consciousness of being held up, sustained within and without, by the divine power; the consciousness, too, of having full possession of all the faculties, and yet losing all thought and sense of death in its ordinary definitions, and feeling that the change through which we are passing is translation rather than dissolution; to feel that slowly, silently, painlessly, we are being lifted out of the body, that the spirit's vision grows clearer and stronger, that we begin to see through the shadows, and far forward and onward through realms of light, almost into the immortal — truly, one who has had this experience comprehends what it is to die — knows

all there is in death, though he may yet live —
and for him

>'Tis easy now to see
> How lovely and how sweet a pass
>   The hour of death may be.
>
> To close the eye, and close the ear,
>   Wrapped in a trance of bliss,
> And, gently drawn in loving arms,
>   To swoon to that — from this:
> Scarce knowing if we wake or sleep,
>   Scarce asking where we are,
> To feel all evil sink away,
>   All sorrow and all care;
>
> While loving spirits hover near,
>   And nestle at our side,
> And into all our thoughts and prayers
>   With gentle helpings glide —
> Then death between us is as naught,
>   A dried and vanished stream —
> Their joy is the reality,
>   Our passing life the dream.

Consolations for the Bereaved.

Blessed be God, even the Father of our Lord Jesus Christ, the Father of mercies, and the God of all comfort; who comforteth us in all our tribulation, that we may be able to comfort them which are in any kind of trouble, by the comfort wherewith we ourselves are comforted of God. — 2 Cor. i. 3, 4.

We will not weep; for God is standing by us,
  And tears will blind us to the blessed sight;
We will not doubt; if darkness still doth try us,
  Our souls have promise of serenest light.
We will not faint; if heavy burdens bind us,
  They press no harder than our souls can bear;
The thorniest way is lying still behind us,
  We shall be braver for our past despair.

O, not in doubt shall be our journey's ending,
  Sin with its fears, shall leave us at the last!
All its best hopes in glad fulfilment blending,
  Life shall be with us still when death is past.
Help us, O Father! when the world is pressing
  On our frail hearts, that faint without their friend;
Help us, O Father! let thy constant blessing
  Strengthen our weakness, — till the joyful end.

I.

The Lessons of Sorrow.

*Deem not that they are blest alone,
Whose days a peaceful tenor keep;
The God who loves our race has shown
A blessing for the eyes that weep.*

IT is a just observation of an eloquent writer, that "sorrow as illustrated in Christ's life, and as interpreted in his scheme of religion, has assumed a new aspect, and yields a new meaning. Its garments of heaviness have become transfigured to robes of light, its crown of thorns to a diadem of glory; and often, for some one whom the rich and joyful of this world pity — some suffering, struggling, overshadowed soul — comes there a voice from heaven, 'This is my beloved son, in whom I am well pleased.'"

It is certainly true, that the suffering and the death of Christ, and the spirit in which they were met and endured, have given a new meaning and dignity to sorrow. And there is something morally grand and beautiful in it, when borne with sweetest patience and serenity of soul, by some frail and feeble sufferer who, but for the example and the religion of Christ, would sink under it into despair; or be irritated into pitiful and useless resistance against that gracious Providence which is forever shaping evil to some beneficent result. And how many have thus been made strong in their weakness by the life and sorrows and death of the blessed Saviour. How many have bowed in willing submission to the divine appointments, and welcomed to their souls the perfect peace of resignation, when they have come to see that they are only treading the path which Jesus trod before them, and trod too for their sake, that they might have courage to go on to the end.

That is a singularly significant and suggestive statement of the apostle: "For ye have not received the spirit of bondage again to fear; but ye have received the spirit of adoption, whereby we cry Abba! Father! The Spirit itself beareth witness with our spirit, that we are the children of God: and if children, then heirs; heirs of God, and joint-heirs with Christ, if so be that we suffer with him, that we may be also glorified together." *If so be that we suffer with him!* Is it not clear from this that suffering is one of the established ordinances of God, with specific reference to our spiritual discipline and exaltation? intended as a means for building up character, and developing our higher nature—in a word, as one of the conditions of our heirship with Christ, "*that we may also be glorified together?*"

And what a remarkable testimony of the Holy Spirit is that which says, "It became him, for whom are all things, and by whom are all things, in bringing many sons unto glory, to make the Captain of their salvation perfect through sufferings." And if it were necessary that Christ should suffer in order to become perfectly fitted for the work to which the Father appointed him, can you expect, my afflicted friend, to be perfect in all things without suffering? Can you spare the lessons of sorrow which it was needful the Son of God should learn, preparatory to his complete consecration? Are you already so trained and strong in spirit that you can spring at once to the loftiest height of heavenly exaltation, without passing through the dark valley marked by the bleeding feet of Jesus? Ah, no — you, and all of us, need the discipline of sorrow and suffering to fit us for the great work of life; to shape into symmetrical proportions the moral and spiritual elements which make up a truly divine character.

And it is one of the first lessons which sorrow teaches, that life is not merely happiness, in the material definition of the term, but virtue, usefulness, character in its largest and best meaning; character as it appears in

Christ; as the symbol of all that is gentle, generous, self-sacrificing and divine. This is the great end of our being; and it is for this that evil is mixed with good, that the shadow of disappointment so often falls athwart the pathway of our enjoyments, that our smiles are sometimes so swiftly veiled in the mist of tears. Afflictions, losses, bereavements, death, are the Lord's angels in disguise, leading us up the heights of celestial perfection and glory. Through them we learn to conquer our weaknesses, to lift our hopes and desires out of the dust of our earthly life, and to set the spirit and its aspirations above the passions and demands of the flesh; till at last we come to feel with the apostles that, "though our outward man perish, yet the inward man is renewed day by day — For our light affliction, which is but for a moment, worketh for us a far more exceeding and eternal weight of glory; while we look not at the things which are seen, but at the things which are not seen: for the things which are seen are temporal, but the things which are not seen are eternal. For we know that if our earthly house of this tabernacle were dissolved, we have a building of God, an house not made with hands, eternal in the heavens."

O child of sorrow! O sad and weary sufferer! what are all your transient griefs compared with this glorious issue? And why should you faint, or murmur, that you must for a little sow the seed in tears, if this be the heavenly fruitage they bear? Why should you accuse the Father, and think that discipline severe which it is in your power to turn into faith and holiness and spirituality?

> If always on the thorns my feet must tread,
> And heavy clouds hang darkly o'er my head;
> If all the sunshine from my life depart,
> And cold, gray ashes be upon my heart;
> If all my hopes, like swift-winged birds, must fly,
> And every flower of promise droop and die;
> If always through a mist of gathering tears
> My eyes watch sadly for the coming years;
> Oh, Father, when Death's river I've passed o'er,
> And my feet stand upon the further shore,
> Shall not Thy seal upon my forehead be,
> "Perfect through suffering," purified by Thee?

II.

The Soul's Hunger and the Bread of Heaven.

Wilt thou not visit me ?
The plant beside me feels thy gentle **dew** ;
Each blade of grass I see,
From thy deep earth its quickening **moisture drew.**
O Lord ! I need thy love
More than the flower the dew, or grass the **rain** ;
Come like thy Holy Dove,
And let me in thy sight rejoice to live again.

THERE is no experience so dreary and desolate, and none so full of promise and hope, as that which, for the first time, reveals to us our spiritual poverty, and the need we have of the bread of God, the heavenly manna which the Gospel provides for the hungry soul. Who has not at times felt weary with himself, dissatisfied with his present condition of mind and heart, deeply conscious that he has not lived as wisely and truly as he should? that he has suffered the world, its gains, and pleasures, and honors, to sweep through his soul like a flood, bearing out from it all thought and love of God? engulfing in the wild rush of muddy waters faith and prayer, mercy and purity, conscience, truth, all the tenderness of his heart, and all the spiritual beauty with which God had fitted up his soul in the beginning? Who does not feel, when all this passes before him as with the swiftness and omnipresence of a dying man's thought, that he has been a traitor to God, and to the noblest dignities of his nature? and, half trembling, for the consequences of this high treason to his soul, and greatly sorrowful for his cold and hard ingratitude to the good God who has loved him through all this with so patient a love — who does not feel springing up within him the prayer of regret and penitence?

Without question this has sometime been

the experience of all who read this. And especially, does this revelation of unworthiness, this dissatisfaction and unrest, come upon them after some great sorrow or bereavement has fallen on them; or when Death has suddenly struck down some dear companion or friend, and the bolt seems scarcely to have missed them. Then this discontent with themselves and the life they are living, then this home-sickness comes upon them with overmastering power — as if a long-forgotten voice, all at once, swept up from the past, calling them tenderly and with the entreating, lingering accents of childhood: "O come back from your long wanderings from the Father — think of his love for you, of what he calls you to, and break from the spell which holds you in bondage to what is so unworthy of you; which keeps you back from the nobler life you are capable of, from the high paths which lead up to the companionship of angels!"

I think we have all heard these voices which call us back to what we were, or forward to what we may be: and have felt this homesickness, this longing after a more righteous life, after something we have not — and preeminently so, when the shadow of a great affliction is over us. Now to this condition of heart, this experience of sorrow, this hunger of the soul in grief, the gospel, in its fulness, brings its word of invitation and encouragement. "Blessed are they that hunger and thirst after righteousness, for they shall be filled." In the quickening truths of the gospel is found precisely what he wants who finds himself in this frame of mind; who feels the long-slumbering affections of his heart now wakening into life, and crying aloud for food, for something which shall supply their clamorous wants. Here, let me say to all such, here in the divine doctrines and precepts of Jesus is found that heavenly manna, that bread of God, which alone can answer to the call of this mighty famine of the soul. Here are the wells of living water, of which if you drink, you will thirst no more forever.

Come to the gospel and you shall find, as no interpreter can tell you, what is the fulness of its blessing. Arise now, and shake the dust of the world from your sandals, and put on the beautiful garments of the spirit, and God shall give you welcome. Set your face towards the Father's house, where there is bread enough and to spare; and the devouring hunger of your heart shall be ministered to, the fatted calf shall be killed, and there shall be joy over you as of one lost but found again — dead once, but now alive forevermore.

If this come to any who have heard these voices, who have seen a white hand beckoning them away to the cool fountains of the gospel, I would entreat them to follow it, till they come to the waters of life. If any experience this hungering and craving for a truer and holier life than they are finding in the dusty streets, in the marts of traffic, in the sharp selfishness of gain-getting, let me say to them, Come, O my brothers, come to the gospel, to the faith, and love, and prayer, which wait to bless you, and to bestow a happiness that will fill the void of your soul. The life of which, now and then, in your better moments, you catch dim glimpses, is real and not a delusion or a dream. The majesty and goodness of God, the worth of truth, the beauty of holiness, the sweet peace of an unaccusing conscience, the royal dignity of a Christian life, and the sublime triumph of the Christian's death; the example of Christ, his great Redemption, the victory of good over every form of evil — these which are the bread of heaven, and the fulness of the gospel blessing, these will meet the yearnings of your heart, will feed its deep hunger, and show you that there is a life — O how much more divine and august than that which is lived only among banks and railroads, ships and merchandise — a life in which the soul, when these shall have perished in the "wreck of matter and the crush of worlds," shall still unfold in ever new and wondrous beauty and power.

O then, my bereaved and sorrowing friend,

let this death which has come so near to you, bring you into closer relations with these great spiritual realities. Let your soul embrace them in a living faith, and appropriate the blessing to itself; and ere long it will rejoice in the new meaning of Christ's words: "I am the bread of life; he that cometh to me shall never hunger, and he that believeth on me shall never thirst." Let this bereavement consecrate your thoughts and affections to higher aims and holier communions; let the life immortal to which your beloved has been translated, become a familiar theme to mind and heart; and by and by you will find the space between earth and heaven bridged over, and the glorified spirits will pass to and fro bringing blessings to your soul, as the angels passed over the shining ladder of Jacob's dream.

> Is a mighty famine now
> In thy heart and in thy soul
> Discontent upon thy brow?
> Turn thee, God will make thee whole.

III.

Through Tribulation into the Kingdom.

Lead us, O Father! to Thy heavenly rest,
However rough and steep the path may be,
Through joy or sorrow, as Thou deemest best,
Until our lives are perfected in Thee.

IF it were left to us, without doubt we should so order our life on earth that it would be all glad and beautiful, bright skies and a green earth, waving forests, and running streams, and lovely landscapes. No clouds should come between us and the sun, no storms should sweep over our path; no disappointments nor griefs should come to us; and sickness and death, and the lone household and the long-sorrowing heart, should be strangers to us and to ours. And so life should be to us a pleasant and merry holiday; and we, like the butterfly or the humming-bird, with bright plumage flashing in the sun, would go dancing from flower to flower, stopping only long enough to gather the honey, and rejoice in the beauty that welcomed us from all sides.

So should we make life, if God would yield to our vain prayers, and suffer our will to be done. And were it so, how worthless would life be to us, and how worthless ourselves also. It is not thus that we get to be strong and worthy of God. The butterfly revels for a season amid beauty and fragrance, but perishes when the winter comes and the storm. But the eagle bravely struggles with the tempest, rises above it, and looks the burning sun in the face with an unflinching eye. So is it with us. Not by the butterfly life, but by the eagle's, we rise up above the storm and the darkness; and the soul, with the keen and strong vision which it has gotten through suffering and faith, is able to behold God and his angels face to face. It is only through this discipline appointed of the Father, that we can be weaned from earth and its influences, and brought into communion with the infinite and the eternal, and the heart made to respond to, and rest in, the blessed truths of the gospel.

And this, after we shall have reasoned as we may, and prayed as we may — this very tribulation and moral training which it is so difficult to accept at God's hand, is the greatest, is the best thing of all for us. Not to urge that it is so since God who is wisest and best has so ordered it, we may, if we will patiently and with a teachable disposition consider it, gather this important truth for ourselves, and so shall it do us greater good.

Who are they who have wrought out great blessings for our race? who have brought forth good unto their fellows, and have left on every spot where they trod a greenness and fragrance which shall never die out? Not they who have been nursed in the lap of luxury and ease — not they whose life has been sunny, and their path amid fresh flowers and over velvet fields. Not these; but they who have been born under clouds; who have grown up amid want, and discouragements, and tribulations; who have toiled up the mountain paths of life, amid wild ravines and beetling crags, facing wind and tempest, amid struggles and perils, till, standing upon the loftiest summit, bathed in sunlight, they see and hear the storm through which they have passed raging far down below them. These are they whom the world calls benefactors, and whom God, having tried, has chosen for his special work. These are they to whom, having passed through much tribulation, the gates of the kingdom of heaven are flung wide open, and free entrance given to its glorious rest.

Paul, though when elected as a servant of God's truth and salvation he had hitherto lived amid wealth and splendor, was trained to his work in the school of suffering, and, taking his life in his hand, went forth amid perils by land and sea, among the heathen and false brethren, amid hunger and thirst and nakedness, stripes and imprisonments, till at last he is able to exclaim, "We glory in tribulations," and to lay down his life for the cause of God and humanity. And it was from the midst of agony in the garden that Christ exclaims, "Not as I will but as thou wilt." And it was from the cross, beneath the cloud of its awful suffering, that the sublime prayer for his murderers went forth, "Father, forgive them." So has it always been. The noblest examples of faith, the most touching exhibitions of love, have had their birth in sorrow and suffering, have come forth like molten gold from the furnace of fire. So in all time the great, the useful have been brought up in the school of trial and adversity. Their weaknesses, their vain longings, the influences of the world and the things that are in it, have given way before the power of

God's discipline, and in their place have come strength and courage, and faith, and love, and heavenly-mindedness.

And do we not all need this discipline to correct what is evil in us, and strengthen what is good? Have we not all weaknesses and earthly longings, and worldliness and sin to overcome, before we can stand by the side of Jesus, of Paul and John? Have we not need, as well as others, to pass through tribulation, before we can enter into the kingdom of God, and take our place with Abraham and Isaac, with James and Peter, and the noble army of martyrs? Ah, yes; we cling to the earth; we cling to the things of the world, we give to them our first and warmest love; we live as though this were our home, as if here only were the proper objects of our affections. And these blessings and gifts — they are ours, and if taken from us in our unworthiness we complain, we have been wronged, and we rebel against the better wisdom of God.

From all this we need to be drawn away, for

while in this state heaven is afar off, and we know not God. While in this state there is no real joy or peace — we know nothing of the higher life of the soul, nor of the kingdom which can now only be reached through much tribulation. And so the Father, who knoweth all this, layeth his hand upon us, and bringeth us into affliction, leadeth us through rough places and dark, into the valley of suffering and humiliation. Disappointment, loss of property, the desertion of friends, crushed hopes, a desolate heart, sickness and death come to us one after another to lay their burthens upon us. The beauty of life departs; the ties that bound us to it have successively been broken. Of those that love us, more are in heaven than here. Old familiar voices are heard no more. The days have come when we say sadly, "We have no pleasure in them;" the shadows have fallen upon the bright places where we have stood, and by and by the dark night gathers about us, and we are alone!

And now our deliverance is at hand. God is not afar. The impatient and murmuring heart is subdued into meekness. We are chastened into submission, and with tearful eye, and a contrite and broken spirit, we pray as we never prayed before. Through the tribulation and suffering which the Father has wisely and mercifully ordered, we are getting forth from the night into day again — we are drawing near to the kingdom of heaven, and its refreshing air comes with a cooling power upon the burning brow, and its sweet peace nestles down upon the weary and throbbing heart — and it is still — at home with God.

Patiently then, and with a sweet submission, let us bear whatsoever the Father may lay upon us. He is wiser than we, and in this way seeks to perfect our spiritual education, and to bring us forth into the infinitely beautiful and blessed life of faith and trust. Let us remember that some of the most fragrant flowers that we ever gather, are taken from the midst of thorns, and often with lacerated and bleeding hands. Our dearest treasures always are bought at the highest price, and mostly are dearest because of the price we pay; for so are they associated with memories that have become sacred through manifold trials and sacrifices. The rainbow, the child of beauty, and the prophet of hope and trust, comes not without the rain. It spans the heavens only when the clouds are there, and from the bosom of the storm looks forth upon us with its placid smile.

With this great truth impressed upon thy heart, therefore, thou poor bereaved one, go forward, leaving God to do for thee and thine whatever to his infinite knowledge and never-changing love may seem best to be done. Be sure what he determines is best. Nothing else will do for thee so desirable and profitable a work as this trial to which God has called thee. It may be severe; the draught may be very bitter; but O, drink it to the last, though thy hand tremble and thy lip quiver. It will do thee good, and thou wilt bless him for it by and by from thy heart of hearts. Thou hast need of the lessons thou art learning. Thou hast found thine own strength to be weakness, and now thou wilt seek to stand in God's strength. Thou hast thought of life only, as if it were forever; now thou wilt think of death, and learn to look it in the face without fear. Thou hast had thy hopes and treasures all on the earth; thou wilt have them in heaven now, and the way will be shorter. Be of cheerful heart then, and faint not, for the Lord is thy refuge, and he will comfort thee.

> "When Israel from his place of shame,
> The Egyptian land of bondage, came,
>   By doubt and terror bowed;
> Tho' legions on her path did pour,
> And trackless waters rolled before,
> God led the host in safety o'er,
>   By pillared fire and cloud.
>
> "So in man's pilgrimage below,
> In all his wandering and woe,
>   See God's sustaining hand;
> His winds breathe o'er the troubled tide,
> His words the opposing waves divide,
> He leads, a never-failing guide,
>   On to the better land."

IV.

Peace in Believing.

And thou, who o'er thy friend's low bier
   Sheddest the bitter drops like rain,
Know that a brighter, happier sphere
   Shall give him to thy arms again.
For God hath marked each anguished day,
   And numbered every secret tear;
And heaven's long age of bliss shall pay
   For all his children suffer here.

WHAT a blessed heritage of strength and trust, of peace and comfort, we have in the gospel of our Lord. What help to us in our weakness, what a soothing balm to the lacerated heart, when the objects of our affection are taken from us, to know that they are, by the mercy of God, lifted into a higher and more blessed life than they could ever have attained to on earth. How it lightens our burthen to feel assured that much as we lose by their death and departure, they gain infinitely more than we lose. We love them; and that is why it is so hard to part with them, why our sorrow is so sharp and keen — we love them; and that is the reason why we struggle against our tears, knowing that they are glorified in heaven. It is for ourselves only that we grieve, not for them; and when we think of all the evils they have escaped, and of all the joys they have won, we feel that it would be selfishness to wish them back again.

We cannot be indifferent to the loss of their society, to our loneliness, to the vacancy in our hearts, to the silence and shadow which brood over the places they filled in our homes. The most perfected Christian on earth must mourn when the precious jewels of his household are taken away, when the objects of his most tender regard are shut from his sight in the cold, dark grave. God knows that we are of the dust, and not of iron. He knows the well-springs of human affection in our hearts, and the pain with which we see a great hope crushed, or a great joy leave us. He does not therefore tell us that we must not sorrow, but only that we should not sorrow as those who are without hope.

"Our Lord Jesus Christ himself, and God, even our Father, which hath loved us, hath given us everlasting consolation and good hope through grace," that we might be strong in the day of bereavement. The resurrection of Christ has shown us that the dear ones who leave us "are not lost, but gone before" to the life immortal; that the body only returns to the dust whence it came, but the spirit to God who gave it! This is the Christian's hope and faith respecting the departed; and he finds comfort, joy even, in his sorrow, persuaded that the dead, the beloved one who has passed "over the river," has gained the crown of immortal life and joy. He can say therefore, in truth,

> "All thy toils and cares are over;
> Weary pilgrim take thy rest;
> God in mercy hath recalled thee
> To thy place among the blest;
> And though now we miss and mourn thee,
> Ours are not despairing tears;
> Well we know we all shall meet thee,
> In a few revolving years."

O how blessed, how beautiful is the Christian faith to the mourner who bends over the dying, or stands at the grave of one who has been loved with deepest tenderness. What a celestial light is sent down into the valley of death by the glad promise of the gospel, the promise that love is immortal, that the affections which bind us so strongly together here cannot be gathered into the grave, cannot die at all. What peace and resignation in the thought, that they who leave us live on as though they had not left us, — nay, do now live more truly than ever before, in a world the glories and the joys of which eye hath not seen, nor the heart conceived.

The transformation which lifts the painfully crawling worm from the dust of the earth into the pure air above it; and, giving it the light and gorgeous wings of the butterfly, sends it glancing through the sunny atmosphere, floating amid beauty and fragrance and gladness, — this is nothing compared to the glorious and heavenly change which death and the resurrection open to the soul, when the body falls away from it, and it rises out of earthly life, on angel wings, into the splendor and joy of the celestial! We cannot estimate the greatness or blessedness of it by any powers of arithmetic, by any severity of logic. Faith only can approach the wealth of its glory, and even with this we see as through a glass darkly; and it is only when we shall have reached the heavenly land itself, and become partakers, that we can understand how great is the heritage of bliss to which our loved ones go, when death leads them away from us.

What a power, then, in the gospel to comfort us, and what a soft light rests on the graves of the departed. We may sometimes go out to them, and we may weep even, but the tears of hope, and of joy even, for the glory the dead have gone to, mingle with the tears of sorrow for our own bereavement. They are not lost to us; they live, and love us still. They have gone to the spirit land only a little before us; and they do not forget us, but expect our coming. There they rejoice,

> "In the broad fields of heaven,
> In the immortal bowers,
> By life's clear river dwelling,
> Amid undying flowers, —
> There hosts of beauteous spirits,
> Fair children of the earth,
> Linked in bright bands celestial,
> Sing of their human birth.
>
> "They sing of earth and heaven, —
> Divinest voices raise
> To God, their gracious Father,
> Who called them to the skies;
> They are all there, — in heaven, —
> Safe, safe and sweetly blest;
> No cloud of sin can shadow
> Their bright and holy rest."

Blessed be God for this blissful assurance of faith, which takes the sting from death, and illumines the gloom of the grave with the morning light of the resurrection; and within it shows us our beloved rejoicing in their new, immortal life; glad forevermore in the smiles of God!

Blessed be the Saviour who has shown us by his own death and triumph that death is conquered, that all whom it has separated shall be reunited in the mansions above. Blessed be his name for the dear promise that,

> "No lingering hope, no parting sigh,
>   Our future meeting knows —
> But love beams forth from every eye,
>   And hope immortal grows, —
> The sacred hope, the blissful hope,
>   Which his rich grace has given;
> The hope when days and years are passed,
>   We all shall meet in heaven!"

V.

Death of Husband or Wife.

"Who never mourned, hath never known what treasures grief reveals —
The sympathies that humanize, the tenderness that heals —
The power to look within the vail and learn the heavenly lore —
The key-word of life's mysteries, so dark to us before."

WHAT a desolation there is in the very sound of this title, the sound which it brings to the heart rather than the ear! When the *Wife* lies cold and still within the coffin, or is carried out from the house that she has made a heaven on earth — the dear being who has from the first commanded all our thoughts and affections, who has been the centre of our aims and ambitions, the thought of whom has made our heaviest toil light, and driven away all weariness, and renewed our youth as the eagle's — O when she is *dead*, when this terrible fact, so hard for us to master at first, breaks in upon us in all its agonizing reality, it is as if the sun had been blotted from out the heavens, and universal night had fallen on the world. What is there now left for us! what happiness is possible in which she has no part? What is home without her who gave it all its worth and joy, whose virtues adorned it, whose smile was its light, and her presence its life?

When the labor or the business of the day is over, how painful and dismal, beyond expression, the return to the domestic sanctuary where she was the idol, the sacred object of our worship; and wandering from room to room, to know and feel that the temple is deserted, and that we are *alone* — alone with our sorrow!

There she used to sit, nestled in that corner, surrounded with the sweet confusion of her needle-work, with the implements and evidences of her pleasing industry — there are her favorite books; and there the instrument over whose keys her facile fingers flew with grace and power, bringing out the most delicious melodies, kindling the soul at will with devotion or delight — everything is in its place, but the presiding spirit, she who gave life to all, is departed forever. What inexpressible grief there is in this crushing thought — *departed forever*, no more to come back to me, no more to welcome me, when the busy day is done, to this home that was so pleasant to us, but now so desolate to me!

So feels and speaks the stricken sufferer whose second self has gone down to the grave, and left him to complete the work, and finish the journey of life alone. And is not all this what we might expect where the blow has lately fallen, and the wound is yet fresh and bleeding? Is it not the natural language of a bereaved and desolate heart?

And so when the wife is called to part with an indulgent and beloved *Husband*. O the anguish and torture which come, when, bending over the dying one, the last convulsive breath is heaved, the last fluttering pulse dies out, and the dear face settles down into the rigidity of death.

And then what hallowed and tender memories come thronging up from the past. In how many thousand ways does her dreadful loss press upon her. And how perpetually, as the days and weeks go by, is she reminded of the happiness which was, but can never be again for her; of the many kindly words and acts which blessed her life. How affectionate and thoughtful he always was. How often his own patience and tender assiduities lifted off the burthen from my heart, and soothed my spirit troubled with household cares, or vexed with social annoyances. However clouded the day, his coming made the evening pleasant and cheerful — and we always went to our rest, the children happy in so kind a father, and I thanking God in my heart for so loving a husband.

He was the strong oak to which I clung as the vine clings to its support; all the tendrils of my life, affections, thoughts, wishes and aims, twining closely around him. I leaned upon him with a sweet and welcome sense of dependence, confident that he would shelter me from all the storms of life, and stand between me and all danger and trouble. There was a blessed sense of security in my thought of him, knowing that in every doubt and difficulty he would guide me, and in my weakness be to me strength and courage. But all this is now passed away; my heart, my hopes, my courage, are buried in the grave with him, and I sink down helpless, crying out with the Psalmist, "O my God, my soul is cast down within me; for all thy waves and thy billows are gone over me."

It would be idle to say that these feelings are unreasonable and wicked. They are natural and inevitable. The merciful God knows this, knows that when we are bereaved in this way, when the beauty of our life perishes, we must suffer and lament for our loss. He does not say "Sorrow not;" but only this, "Sorrow not as those *who are without hope.*" We are not without hope; not without *faith*, that under his direction all things come to pass for some wise and beneficent end; that evil and good, grief and joy, death and life, are equally the ministers of his mercy. And you, sad and unhappy mourner, who just now repeated the anguish cry of the Psalmist — you should have gone a little farther, and heard him afterward, from the deeps of his affliction, lifting up the sublime prayer of resignation and trust: "All thy waves and thy billows are gone over me, *yet* the Lord will command his loving-kindness in the day-time, and in the night his song shall be with me, and my prayer unto the God of my life. . . . Why art thou cast down, O my soul? and why art thou disquieted within me? hope thou in God; for I shall yet praise him, who is the health of my countenance and my God."

This was the faith of David in the most

grievous trial of his life; and why should it not be yours? Was the Jewish dispensation clearer than the Christian is in regard to the beneficent purpose of evil? Did the Psalmist look at death and the world beyond from a higher stand-point than the true disciple of him who, "through death, destroyed death," and "brought life and immortality to light?" It is a sore affliction, this loss of yours; but then how great is the comfort wherewith God comforteth all those who are in any kind of trouble. How precious

> "The hope, the blissful hope,
> Which Jesus' grace hath given;
> The hope when days and years are past,
> We all shall meet in heaven."

Beside, ought you not to temper the passionateness of your grief, by remembering that you knew all this in the day when you gave your heart to your beloved. You knew that you were not always to live together on earth; that you and your companion must die, each one at the time appointed, and that one of you must die first. And now think for a little calmly: you know what you who remain suffer by this separation; and you believe without doubt that it is well with the departed, that the bliss of heaven is attained. Do you then wish that you had gone first, and that your companion had been left to suffer all the anguish which wrings your heart, to experience the terrible loneliness which oppresses you, and to bear the heavy burthen of life unblessed by the sweet sympathy of kindred affection? This must, from the necessity of the case, be the lot of one of you; and, loving as you do, if the choice had been given you, to which would you have assigned it? O is it not better, then, as God has ordered it? When seen from this point of view, can you not say, "Thy will, O God, be done!" Since the separation must come, since *one* must bear the sharp pain of bereavement, and walk in darkness and solitude, would you not rather choose it for yourself, than for the object of your affection? Is not this the magnanimity of true, unselfish love?

And then, on the other hand, consider the glory of that translation which has lifted your companion out of the earthly into the heavenly. Think not that this is only a kind effort to comfort you; it is the grandest fact of the Christian revelation, this freedom and growth, this immortal joy to which our beloved go when they pass "over the river." And surely, if our affection for them is what it should be, wise and unselfish, how great soever the loss to us, we should rejoice for their sake. One who has spoken well on this point, says:—

"We blame no one that for his own sake he feels the pangs of separation, but we do wonder that there is no more generosity in the love which we bear to our dear ones; and that the full and glorious certainties which illumine their condition when they have passed beyond us, do not cast back some light of joy upon our grief! We mourn as those who have no hope; whereas our mightiest griefs should be imbosomed in hope and calm certainties of joy. What copious tears we shed because God will bring up our babes for us! With what frantic sorrow do we beat ourselves because our heart-companions are suddenly translated into all honor, and nobleness, and purity, and ecstacy of joy! When the golden gate is opened, and our beloved ones pass through, we may be sad that we are left in the drear wilderness, but not that they have entered the city of their coronation! If we could but break down by our faith and imagination the barrier which our senses interpose; if we could but walk the garden-road, and move through the celestial air, beholding the fulfilment of the earthly promise, witnessing the perfection of what we know in error and confusion; if we could but assure ourselves of the lustrous beauty, the glorious largeness and liberty, the wonderful purity and joy of those whom God hath called and crowned with immortality; unless we were petrified with selfishness, we should lay aside our sorrow in overmeasure, and break forth with thanksgiving. Since only days and weeks are between us and those who have gone before, since joy and sorrow alike, and the whole course of earthly experiences, are bearing us straight onward to the same abode, it would seem the very wantonness of unregulated grief not to find consolation and patience, yea, and a sobered gladness, that we are known in heaven by our forerunners!"

> The mourners came at break of day
>   Unto the garden-sepulchre,
> With sorrowing hearts to weep and pray
>   For him whom they had buried there.
> What radiant light dispels the gloom?
> An angel sits beside the tomb!
>
> Then mourn we not beloved dead—
>   E'en while we come to weep and pray
> The happy spirit far hath fled
>   To brighter realms of endless day!
> Immortal hope dispels the gloom;
> An angel sits beside the tomb!

VI.

Comfort the Children.

O comfort the little ones ; think of their grief,
   When Death bears the mother away ;
Forget thine own sorrow to bring them relief,
   And teach the young heart how to pray —
O lead the poor lambs to the Shepherd above,
And leave them to rest in the arms of his love.

IN reply to what is said in the preceding section, you may answer that you *are* thankful for the faith which reveals an inheritance of liberty and joy for the departed; but that your own loss, which is heavy enough, is made doubly so by the sorrow of dear children who have been deprived of a dear parent. Yes, but have not these children a claim upon you for help and consolation? Is it not a duty, as far as is in your power, to master your own sorrow, that you may minister unto theirs? They are young and helpless — perhaps this is their first great grief. Their thoughts of God and his providence, of life and death, of the present and the future, are not as matured as yours; their faith is not yet ripened, and they cannot lean upon it for support and comfort. It is their privilege, therefore, to look to the surviving parent for that sweet and intelligent sympathy which equally soothes and sustains. Death is a mystery to them — and Heaven and the spiritual existence? they are afar off, and lie vaguely in their thought. They need the instruction and guidance of a parent's loving heart, that their grief may be assuaged, their tears dried, and their eyes lifted toward the realms of light. Comfort them, then, and help to lift the shadow from their hearts, and to lead them in the way of life everlasting.

Is it a Father who has gone from them? Then for their sake, O Mother, control your grief, and teach and console them by hopeful words, by an humble Christian resignation, and by lifting their thoughts from death to the Life Immortal, from the temporary separations of earth to the eternal re-unions of Heaven. Inspire them with cheerful views touching the discipline of sorrow, the mission of death, and the glory and ineffable happiness of the world beyond the river. Through this bereavement lead their hearts to God and the Saviour, and help them to feel that they have a Father in heaven, whose providential care enfolds them, whose love blesses them, and whose divine law is their safe and sure road to usefulness, honor, and abiding peace. In this way you will comfort them and comfort yourself; you will keep the head and the heart busy in the beautiful work of parental culture, and soothe to rest the bitter thoughts which otherwise will fling their gloom over all your life. And in what way better than this can you honor the memory of their father, or secure the loving smile of approbation from the glorified spirit of your husband in heaven?

Is it a Mother of whom these children have been bereaved? Ah, then, my brother, what great, yet pleasing, duties fall to your lot, if you would make good the place of one who, of all others, is necessarily nearest and dearest to the lambs of the flock. Sorrowfully is this impressed upon you; and you are ready to say, as dear as she was to you, and great as is the anguish caused by her death, that the sharpest pain comes when you think of the children deprived of a mother, a mother who, in joy and sorrow, in health and sickness, was their guide, their refuge, their comforter, their all.

But what a sweet relief to your overburthened heart, when, as the evening comes on, remembering her last words, and all the earnest longings of the mother's heart, you sit and talk with them of her; and recount all her virtues, all her wishes and prayers in their behalf, and all her hopes and aims respecting their future. Will not the hours devoted to this grateful service be blessed to your own consolation, and establish a holy communion between you and the spirit of their sanctified mother? In leading their thoughts up to her, will not your own heart go with them? Will not heaven become more real to you, and her spirit seem nearer, *and be nearer*, and more visible to the clairvoyant eye of faith? And will not your grief pass away in this blessed fellowship of soul? and the glory of the future be reflected back through all the gloom of the present? And so, for this, will your heart draw nigh to the dear Saviour, who suffered and died, that we might have this "strong consolation," this "hope which is as an anchor of the soul, both sure and steadfast, entering into that within the veil." And thus will it be revealed to you, how all our trials and griefs and bereavements clothe themselves at last in garments of light; and become, as it were, rounds in the shining ladder by which we climb up to God and heaven.

The following exceedingly beautiful and touching lines, written some time since by one who was approaching the banks of the river, are a most eloquent and effective expression of this thought. They bear the title of "The Dying Wife and Mother."

Lay the gem upon my bosom, let me feel her sweet, warm breath,
For a strange chill o'er me passes, and I know that it is death;
I would gaze upon the treasure, scarcely given, before I go;
Feel her rosy, dimpled fingers wander o'er my cheek of snow.

I am passing through the waters, but a blessed shore appears;
Kneel beside me, husband, dearest, let me kiss away thy tears;
Wrestle with thy grief, my husband, strive from midnight until day;
It may prove an angel's blessing when it vanishes away.

Lay the gem upon my bosom, 'tis not long she can be there;
See! how to my heart she nestles — 'tis the pearl I love to wear;
If in after years beside thee, sits another in my chair —
Though her voice be sweeter music, and her face than mine more fair;

If a cherub call thee father, far more beautiful than this,
Love my first-born! oh, my husband! turn not from the motherless.
Tell her sometimes of her mother — you can call her by my name;
Shield her from the winds of sorrow — if she errs, oh, gently blame!

COMFORT THE CHILDREN.

Lead her sometimes where I'm sleeping, I will answer if she calls;
And my breath will stir her ringlets, when my voice in blessing falls;
And her soft blue eyes will brighten, and she'll wonder whence it came —
In her heart when years pass o'er her, she will find her mother's name.

It is said that every mortal walks between two angels here;
One records the ill, but blots it, if before the midnight drear
Man repenteth; if uncanceled then, he seals it for the skies,
And the right hand angel weepeth, bowing low with veiled eyes.

I will be her right hand angel, sealing up the good for heaven,
Striving that the midnight watches find no misdeed unforgiven;
You will not forget me, husband, when I'm sleeping 'neath the sod,
Love the jewel God has given us, as I love thee, next to God.

VII.

The Death of Children.

> Gone, we know not from what suffering,
> Fled, we know not from what sin —
> O ye gates that open heavenward,
> Swing together, shut them in!

A SAD thing it is when a little child dies, sad for the loving parents, sad for the child's brothers and sisters, sad for all the household. It was a sweet little prattler, the joy of the mother's heart, the hope and pride of the father, and the delight of all the children. It was so gentle and loving, so winning in its ways, so intelligent and observing; it filled so large a space in the thoughts, and cares, and affections of the mother; it was in so many places about the house, it put so many things into disorder by its frolicsome mirth, its sweet voice made such music everywhere, it was so much company, it uttered such wise sayings and such great words, and asked so many and such strange questions; why it seems, when it went away, as if it took the whole house with it, as if everything was gone, and only silence and sorrow left.

Or it may be that your child was no longer a *little* child, but had passed on to half a score or more of years — a pleasant, manly, robust boy, full of life, full of generous impulses, genial, affectionate, ambitious, always hopeful and happy, making the house merry with his songs and jests, —

Or, perhaps, the opposite of this in some things, he might have been a quiet, thoughtful, retiring lad; never very strong, never fond of the rough sports of boys brimming over with animal life; loving the house better than the street, fond of his books, living a kind of dreamy life, often speaking of religious things, asking mother strange questions of

God and heaven and angels and the dead; all his thoughts and conversation, the pale spiritual face, and the frail and feeble body, prophetic of an early departure, —

Or, the dear child that has left you may have been a gentle and loving daughter; one of those sweet children we sometimes see, who seem as if they had strayed from heaven, and unknowingly found their way down to earth; and, with a half-homesick feeling, were waiting patiently for the Messenger to come and take them home again. She went about the house so lightly and pleasantly, that she seemed to float like a spirit rather than to walk; a soft smile ever lighting up her expressive features, never without a flower in her hand or in her hair, or somewhere about her dress; secreted oftentimes for hours alone in some hidden corner, in the house, in the garden, among the shrubbery, murmuring in low voice some pleasant strain of music, reading, or fondling some pet; or perhaps wholly absorbed in thoughts beyond her years, —

Of such sort as one of these may have been the child that Death has taken in his arms and borne away from you — and O what a difference it has made in your home and your heart! How it has changed the tone and color of your thoughts, and taken the warmth and beauty out of your life, and darkened all the hopes and ambitions that were linked in with the future of the beloved child. How tasteless and unsatisfying is all pleasure, how dull and uninteresting the book you are reading, how little you sympathize in the idle talk of your visitors, how everything in the world has lost its point and meaning for you.

But, after all, is this as it should be? Is this such an expression of confidence and submission toward your Heavenly Father, as he is entitled to? Is this a state of mind and heart becoming a Christian believer? And does it show that self-appropriation of the blessed promises of God, and of the sweet consolations of Christ, which we have a right to expect from one who has so long enjoyed the benefits of religious instruction, and all the privileges of the Lord's sanctuary?

Has not God taken the child you love so tenderly to heaven, to immortal life and blessedness? and does not your grief therefore border on the selfish? Do you not lose sight of what your child has gained, in your blind lamentation for what you have lost? Surely "it is well with the child," and ought not this to soothe you and comfort you? It is lifted out of all sorrow and suffering forevermore, and is not this something to be thankful for? Why then this utter desolation of heart, this weeping as though nothing were left you to be thankful for?

It is said of the lady of Sir Stamford Raffles, in India, that she was overwhelmed with grief for the loss of a favorite child, and was unable to bear even the light of day. She was lying on her couch, with a feeling of desolation that was fast growing into despair, when she was addressed by a poor, ignorant woman, one of the native converts, who had been employed in the nursery: "I am come," said the woman, "because you have been here many days shut up in a dark room, and no one dares to come near you. Are you not ashamed to grieve in this manner, when you ought to be thanking God for having given you the most beautiful child that ever was seen? Did any one ever see him or speak of him without admiring him? And instead of letting this child remain in this world till he should be worn out with trouble and sorrow, has not God taken him to heaven in all his beauty? For shame! leave off weeping, and let me open a window."

What a lesson there is here for you! How much is there in that thought, that perhaps the child is taken away from the evil to come. At any rate, now there are no more anxieties in this regard on your part, no more fears nor tremblings lest it may be the prey of disease, or fall into evil, or be led away into some temptation. All this is over now; the pure-minded and generous boy, the gentle and lovely girl, are safely removed from all these perils; and in all their freshness and beauty, before they knew any real wrong or sorrow, they are walking with the angels.

>They at least are safe from falling
> On the battle-field of life,
>Overcome, as thousands have been
> By temptation, care, and strife;
>And have died with hands close gathered
> In the tender clasp of ours —
>God be thanked that we could fold them
> Pure as snow, and full of flowers!
>
>So, with Love's divinest token,
> Yielded to a tenderer care
>Than the home below could give them,
> Or our human weakness bear,
>They are safe from pain and sorrow;
> Cheerfully we'll bear the rod,
>With these blossoms safely nurtured
> In the garden of our God.

But they were so dear to us, so young and beautiful, just opening into life; and they would have been such a comfort and a joy to us if they had lived — we cannot help mourning for their death; it is so hard to see the sweet blossoms wither and fall. Yes, this is true; and it brings to me another thought which has sometimes risen within me, when meditating on the death of children. I have compared them to young trees in a nursery, set out only for a time, for the express purpose of being removed, and at the fitting season transplanted to another and more suitable place, where they may grow into symmetry, beauty and fruitage, without hindrance or interruption. Is it not so with children, transplanted from earth to heaven, only that they may grow into larger life, and expand into greater beauty and glory, free from all the defects and imperfections of this lower world? And is it not with God, as with the gardener, that he sometimes, for special reasons, selects the fairest, the most symmetrical and promising for removal and transplantation?

But let us hear again a writer already quoted, who says in the true spirit of resignation and faith,

"When God gives me a babe, I say, 'I thank God for this lamp lit in my family.'

And when, after it has been a light in my household for one or two years, it pleases God to take it away, I can take the cup bitter or sweet: I can say, 'My light is gone out; my heart is sacked; my hopes are desolated; my child is lost — my child is lost!' or I can say in the spirit of Job, 'The Lord gave, and the Lord hath taken away; blessed be the name of the Lord.' It has pleased God to take five children from me; but I never *lost* one, and never shall. When I have a child that Christ covets, with a divine coveting, and he says to me, in words of tenderness, 'Will you not give me the child, and let me take care of it, instead of yourself?' my flesh may remonstrate, but my heart says, 'Lord, take it and adopt it.' I have lived long enough since the taking away of my children, to find that it is better as it is, than that they should have remained with me.

"As believers in Christianity, which reveals God as our Father, and heaven as our eternal home, it is our privilege to feel that when our children are taken from us, they are not *lost* to us, but only pass on before us to the spirit world, to become angelic beings around the burning throne of God and the Lamb. Jesus declared that of such is the kingdom of heaven. They have gone up to live with the crowned immortals, to be watched for and cared for by the angels of light, and we doubt not that they will be among the first to welcome us among the shining courts on High."

What a pleasing and consoling truth, that the little one whom you folded to your heart with such fervent tenderness, is waiting over the river to welcome you with even greater affection, greater because it is divine and everlasting. How delightful the thought that you have a child in heaven! Perhaps hitherto heaven has been in your thought as a kind of foreign land, afar off, in which you had little or no interest, and about which you had no desire to hear. You had no friends there; no member of your family was a dweller in that seemingly distant region; no treasure of yours was laid up there.

But now, how different! Now, that your dear child has gone to reside there, heaven is no longer a foreign country, no longer afar off, but near to you. And you think of it constantly, and love to hear and talk about it, and when the time comes you will go with sweet anticipations of meeting, and being welcomed by, your angel child.

"Sometime ago," says a pleasing writer, "I was at the funeral of the child of a pastor; and when the neighboring minister, who had been called to bury his brother's child, had closed his words of sympathy and comfort, the stricken father rose — the house in which we were assembled stood on a hillside, overlooking a beautiful river, and on the other side 'sweet fields stood dressed in living green.'" The pastor went on to say — and there was a strange power and beauty in the words as they fell from his lips in the midst of tears — "Often, as I have stood on the borders of this stream, and looked over to the fair fields on the other shore, I have felt but little interest in the people or the place in full view before me. The river separates me from them, and my thoughts and affections were here. But a few months ago one of my children moved across to the other side, and took up his residence there. Since that time my heart has been there also. In the morning when I rise and look out toward the east, I think of my child who is over there; and again and again through the day I think of him, and the other side of the river is always in my thoughts with the child who has gone there to dwell. And now since another of my children has crossed the river of death, and has gone to dwell on the other side, my heart is drawn out toward heaven and the inhabitants of heaven, as it was never drawn before. I supposed that heaven was dear to me; that my Father was there, and my friends were there, and that I had a great interest in heaven — *but I had no child there!* Now I have; and I never think and never shall think of heaven, but with the memory of that dear child who is to be among its inhabitants forever."

In the Scottish hills as a Shepherd strolled
   In the eve with his ancient crook,
He found a lamb that was young and chilled
   By the side of a purling brook.

And fearing the lamb might sicken and die —
   Or from its mother's side might roam —
He carried it up with a tender care
   To a fold in his highland home.

'Mid the dreary night — o'er the craggy peaks —
   Through the winds, and the storms and cold,
The mother followed her captured lamb
   To the door of the Shepherd's fold.

Once we had a lamb by its mother's side —
   It was artless and pure and mild —
The dearest lamb in our own dear flock,
   Was the pale little blue-eyed child!

But a shepherd came when the sun grew low,
   By a path that has long been trod,
And carried our lamb through the mists of night,
   To his fold in the Mount of God.

With a tearful eye and a bleeding heart,
   We must bear it and struggle on;
Must climb the mount by the Shepherd's track,
   To the fold where our lamb is gone.

VIII.

The Memory of the Dead.

> The departed! the departed!
>   They visit us in dreams;
> And they glide above our memories,
>   Like shadows over streams:
> We know that they are happy,
>   With their angel plumage on,
> But our hearts are very desolate
>   To think that they are gone.

IN almost every household there is cherished the memory of some dear soul that has gone out to return no more. The mother tenderly remembers her babe; the father thinks regretfully of his manly son, whose youth was so full of promise; the children grieve for the loss of a sweet and gentle sister, or a dear brother, a brave and generous boy, whose faults are all forgotten, and his virtues all remembered. In every home there is an enshrined memory, a sacred relic, a ring, a lock of shining hair, a broken plaything, a book, a picture, something sacredly kept and guarded, which speaks of death, which tells as plainly as words, of some one long since gone. For, truly,

> There is no flock, however watched and tended,
> But one dead lamb is there!
> There is no fireside, howsoe'er defended,
> But has one vacant chair!

It is one of the most beautiful traits of our humanity, this tender memory of the dead; this quick forgetfulness of all that was unpleasant, and this eager calling up of every grace and beauty, of every gentle and winning thing in the character and life of the departed. Some one has truly said: "Let death take from the household the troublesome and ungovernable child, and all that is remembered is his sweet and gentle words, his rare qualities, his loving way, his beauty and manliness. The child stands before his parent's eyes, not as what he was, but as what he might have been had all God put in him been perfected by love and grace. He is now always 'dear child' in their thought, and no longer selfish and unlovely. The children long for their dead companion with real and tender grief — they would be pleasanter were he back again; they are surprised to find how much they loved him. Friends long to have the opportunity, now lost, to show their love. Why did I not prize him more — why did I not serve him better, is the universal feeling."

And this is equally true of all, as well as of children. Death seems to sanctify all our thoughts of the departed; we willingly forget the evil, and remember only the good there was in them. There is a sweet expression of this feeling, this sacred memory of the dead, in a passage from Washington Irving, which follows:

"The sorrow for the dead is the only sorrow from which we refuse to be divorced. Every other would we seek to heal — every other affliction to forget; but this wound we consider it a duty to keep open—this affliction we cherish and brood over in solitude. Where is the mother who would willingly forget the infant that perished like a blossom from her arms, though every recollection is a pang? Where is the child who would willingly forget the most tender of parents, though to remember be but to lament? Who, even in the hour of agony, would forget the friend over whom he mourns? Who, even when the tomb is closing upon the remains of her he most loved, when he feels his heart as it were, crushed in the closing of its portal, would accept of consolation that must be bought by forgetfulness? No; the love which survives the tomb is one of the noblest attributes of the soul. It has its woes, it likewise has its delights; and when the overwhelming burst of grief is calmed into the gentle tear of recollection—when the sudden anguish and the convulsive agony over the present ruins of all that we most loved, is softened away into pensive meditation on all that it was in the days of its loveliness — who would root out the sorrow from the heart? Though it may sometimes throw a passing cloud over the bright hour of gayety, or spread a deeper sadness over the hour of gloom, yet who would change it even for the song of pleasure, or the burst of revelry? No; there is a voice from the tomb sweeter than song. There is a remembrance of the dead, to which we turn even from the charms of the living. Oh, the grave! the grave! It buries every error — covers every defect, extinguishes every resentment! From its peaceful bosom spring none but fond regrets and tender recollections."

Who that has ever been bereaved has not realized this in his own experience; and felt that there is a sorrow better for him, dearer to him, than any joy the world can give. Who that has ever lost a beloved one, a child, a parent, a friend, has not sometime realized that, dead, they have become more to him than they ever could have been living — nay, that, dead, they have done more for him, blessed him more, lifted him nearer to God and the heavenly life, than they could ever have done while in the body. O yes, the memory of the dead often has for us a sanctifying power which the presence of the living, however sweet their communion, never had; and in our frequent thought of them, we find that our hearts and hopes are slowly disentangling themselves from the earthly, and steadily drifting heavenward.

"How beautiful is the memory of the dead! What a holy thing it is in the human heart, and what a chastening influence it sheds upon human life! How it subdues all the harshness that grows up within us in the daily intercourse with the world! How it melts our unkindness, softens our pride, kindling our deepest love, and waking our highest aspirations! Is there one who has not some loved friend gone into the eternal world, with whom he delights to live again in memory?

Does he not love to sit down in the hushed and tranquil hours of existence, and call around him the face, the form, so familiar and cherished?

"The blessed dead! how free from stain is our love for them! The earthly taint of our affections is buried with that which was corruptible, and the divine flame in its purity illumines our breast. We have now no fear of losing them. They are fixed for us eternally in the mansions prepared for our re-union. Our hearts are sanctified by their words which we remember. How wise they have now grown in the limitless fields of truth. How joyous they have become by the undying fountains of pleasure. The immortal dead! how unchanging is their love for us. How tenderly they look down upon us, and how closely they surround our being. How earnestly they rebuke the evil of our lives.

"Let men talk pleasantly of the dead, as those who no longer suffer and are tried — as those who pursue no longer the fleeting, but have grasped and secured the real. With them the fear and the longings, the hope, and the terror, and the pain are past: the fruition of life has begun. How unkind, that when we put away their bodies, we should cease the utterance of their names. The tender-hearted dead who struggled so in parting from us! why should we speak of them in awe, and remember them only with sighing? Very dear were they when hand clasped hand, and heart responded to heart. Why are they less dear when they have grown worthy a higher love than ours, and their perfected souls might receive even our adoration! By their hearth-side, and by their grave-side, in solitude, and amid the multitude, think cheerfully and speak lovingly of the dead."

> "The dead are like the stars by day,
> Withdrawn from mortal eye,
> Yet holding unperceived their way
> Through the unclouded sky.
> By them, through holy hope and love,
> We feel in hours serene
> Connected with a world above,
> Immortal and unseen."

IX.

The Dead never Grow Old.

> Many years the dust hath lain
>   Smoothly o'er that marble face,
> And the busy world without
>   Of his presence bears no trace;
> But in faithful hearts he lives,
>   Young as when on earth he trod,
> Though a holy spirit now,
>   Standing by the throne of God.

THE dead are the only people who never grow old. The man of four-score years and more remembers his father and mother as they were in his youth or childhood. If they died when he had numbered only half a score of years, he does not in his thought of them add to their age the three-score and ten years which he has lived since. At eighty they are the same to him as when he was ten;

they have not changed at all since the day they died. Through all the toils and conflicts and sorrows of seventy years, the sweet face of his sainted mother has hung in the portrait gallery of his memory, as fresh and fair as when he took his last look of her.

That manly and graceful youth, though he died long time ago, is the same in the thought of his father; every lineament, every look, every expression of the face. The father himself has grown old, and is beginning to bend under the weight of years; but the son is still a young man, as fair in look, as erect in form, as elastic in step, as ever—and he will always be so to his father.

And so with the mother and her babe. The child dies, and is always a child thenceforth. Half a century may go by, but it adds nothing to the age of the little prattler, who left her far back as long ago as that. Leigh Hunt says, with truth, that "those who have lost an infant are never, as it were, without an infant child. They are the only persons who, in one sense, retain it always, and they furnish their neighbors with the same idea. The other children grow up to manhood and womanhood, and suffer all the changes of mortality. This one is rendered an immortal child. Death has arrested it with his kindly harshness, and blessed it into an eternal image of youth and innocence." And the words of Ainsworth are as truthful as they are beautiful, when he says, "the little boy that died, so long ago, is an eternal child; and even as he crept over the threshold of God's gates ajar at the beckoning of the Lord; so ever in the heart his parting look, with heaven shining full upon his brow, the beauty that the heart grew warm beholding, remains untouched by time, even as the unrent sky that let the wanderer in."

This is one of God's kindly compensations for the loss which death inflicts. The bereaved only have friends who never change. The fair-haired lad who went away in the flower of his age, never grows to manhood or age in the memory of his brothers or sisters; and the gentle girl who fell asleep in death, however long ago, still holds her place in their hearts, as young, as gladsome, as winning, as lovely as before the angel called her. The opening bud remains in all its beauty and sweetness; and it will never pass into the full-blown rose, and fade and droop, and cast its withered leaves to the earth.

The Country Parson has a passage which illustrates this peculiar feature in our thought of the dead:

"Your little brother or sister, that died long ago, remains in death, and in remembrance the same young thing forever. It is fourteen years this evening since the writer's sister left this world. She was fifteen years old then — she is fifteen years old yet. I have grown older since by fourteen years, but she has never changed as they advanced; and if God spares me to four-score, I never shall think of her as other than the youthful creature she was when she faded. The other day

I listened as a poor woman told of the death of her first-born child. He was two years old. She had a small washing-green, across which was stretched a rope that came, in the middle, close to the ground. The boy was leaning on the rope, swinging backwards and forwards, and shouting with delight. The mother went into her cottage, and lost sight of him for a minute; and when she returned the little man was lying across the rope, dead. It had got under his chin: he had not sense to push it away; and he was suffocated.

"But the thing which mainly struck me was, that though it is eighteen years since then, the mother thought of her child as an infant of two years yet: it is a little child she looks for to meet her at the gate of the Golden City. Had her child lived he would have been twenty years old now; he died, and he is only two: he is two yet; he will never be more than two. The little rosy face of that morning, and the little half-articulate voice, would have been faintly remembered by the mother had they gradually died into boyhood and manhood; but that day stereotyped them: they remain unchanged."

The poem which follows is a tender expression of this thought; and reveals the pleasing fact, that the "little maiden," dying, is always a little maiden, and the "little vacant chair" ever after sacred to her memory.

> Still my heart and eyes are turning
> To a little vacant chair,
> Standing idly in the corner —
> Ever standing idly there:
> Once it held a little maiden,
> Very dear and very fair.
>
> In the fullest tide of rapture,
> In my life's serenest hour,
> When my spirit sang within me
> Like a bird in summer bower.
> Came a tempest sweeping o'er me,
> Came with desolating power.
>
> Then a voice of tender sweetness
> Died away in plaintive sighs,
> Then a face of gentle beauty
> Faded from my yearning eyes,
> And a spirit pure and sinless
> Mounted to its native skies.

Oh! the sorrow of that moment;
  Oh! the weary, weary pain,
Pressing, like an iron fetter,
  Close on throbbing heart and brain,
Waking thoughts of gloom and madness
  Like the captive's heavy chain.

Years have passed, and grief's wild torrent
  Now hath slowly ebbed away;
Years have passed, and resignation,
  Smiling, bids me trust and pray;
Yet a memory, sad and sacred,
  Trembles at my heart alway.

Ever as the shades of twilight
  Wrap the world in tender gloom,
Comes a welcome, fairy vision,
  Stealing to my lonely room—
Seeming, like a ray of sunshine,
  All the darkness to illume.

Then the little chair beside me
  Rocketh softly to and fro;
Then fond eyes to mine are lifted;
  Then sweet accents round me flow,
Till again my dreaming spirit
  Drinks the bliss of long ago.

X.

"The Valley of Peace," or the Place of the Dead.

"They shall be Mine." O, lay them down to slumber,
　Calm in the strong assurance that he gives;
He calls them by their names, he knows their number,
　And they shall live as surely as he lives.

THE Scriptural record in Genesis xxiii. is pleasantly related to the title of this section: "And the field of Ephron, which was in Machpelah, which was before Mamre, the field, and the cave which was therein, and all the trees that were in the field, that were in all the borders round about, were made sure unto Abraham, for a possession of a burying-place by the sons of Heth." It is worthy of note, the care which was taken at this early period to secure suitable and pleasant places for the burial of the dead. It is easy to see that the spot selected by the patriarch was retired, rural and pleasant to the eye. Not only the cave is mentioned, but the field, or rural district, in which it is situated; and special mention is made of the trees, not only in the field itself, but those also that were "in all the borders round about." It would seem as if special contract had been made by Abraham that the border trees should be spared, or be left standing, to add to the beauty, the quiet, and agreeableness of the place where his dead were to be laid to their rest.

And we find it afterward recorded that his family were buried in this lovely cemetery; his son, and his son's son, and their wives. When Jacob drew nigh unto death he charged his sons, saying, "I am to be gathered unto my people: bury me with my fathers in the cave that is in the field of Machpelah, which is before Mamre, in the land of Canaan, which Abraham bought for a possession of a burying-place. There they buried Abraham and Sarah his wife; there they buried Isaac and Rebecca his wife; and there I buried Leah. And when Jacob had made an end of commanding his sons, he gathered up his feet into the bed, and yielded up the ghost, and was gathered unto his people."—Gen. xlix. 29.

The Jews, and eastern nations generally, had their burial-places and tombs in the fields, at a distance beyond the city walls, in gardens, on the sides of the hills — in any secluded and pleasant spot which taste or affection might fix upon as grateful to the eye, or soothing to the mourning heart. And into this chosen and sacred place were gathered evergreens, and flowers, and shrubbery; and these were vocal with the ever varying melodies of the forest songsters.

Aside from any opinions respecting the future life of the departed, or the resurrection from the dead, this custom carries with it a pleasant look, and cannot but have a softening and refining influence over the living. It secures one spot to sacred thought and holy memories. It keeps the chain of remembrance bright, and links us more closely with the dead; and so beautifies the heart with an ever fresh affection, and a perpetually growing religious tenderness. It makes the grave not a place of gloom and despair, not the quickener of tears and bitter sighs; but, with its flowers and fragrance, its spring-tide greenness and renovation, a teacher of better hopes, and a symbol of the resurrection.

And so it becomes in the wide wilderness of life a kind of oasis, cool and quiet, where we rest awhile on the journey homeward to heaven and our Father. The associations which gather about it are of a subdued and cheerful character. The pleasant light of the sun falls softly upon the perfumed bed where our loved ones have lain down to sleep after the weary march of life. The grand old trees, with their rich foliage, and long waving arms, bend over it kindly; while the winds murmur plaintive strains among the leaves and branches. The odorous breath of flowers is there, and their sweet faces look up smilingly and hopefully from the grave sod. The birds come and sing to the sleepers, and almost we can fancy that their delicious melody sometimes floats into the dreams of our precious ones, and recalls the hours when we used to wander with them beneath the forest trees, and listen to the glad notes of the happy songsters.

There is a beautiful incident mentioned by an eastern traveller, of which I am reminded here :—

At Smyrna, the burial ground of the Armenians, like that of the Moslem, is removed a short distance from the town, is sprinkled with green trees; and is a favorite resort, not only with the bereaved, but with those whose feelings are not thus darkly overcast. I met there one morning a little girl, with a half-playful countenance, busy blue eye, and sunny locks, bearing in one hand a small cup of china, and in the other a wreath of fresh flowers. Feeling a very natural curiosity to know what she could do with these bright things in a place which seemed to partake so much of sadness, I watched her light motions. Reaching a retired grave covered with a plain marble slab, she emptied the seed — which it appeared the cup contained — into the slight cavities which had been scooped out in the corners of the level tablet, and laid the wreath on its pure face.

"And why," I inquired, "my sweet girl, do you put seed in those little bowls there?"

"It is to bring the birds here," she replied with a half-wondering look; "they will light on this tree when they have eaten the seed, and sing."

"To whom do they sing, to you or to each other?"

"Oh no!" she replied, "to my sister — she sleeps here."

"But your sister is dead?"

"Oh yes, sir, but she hears the birds sing."

"Well, if she does hear the birds sing, she cannot see that wreath of flowers."

"But she knows I put it there. I told her, before they took her away from our house, I would come and see her every morning."

"You must," I continued, "have loved that sister very much; but you will never talk with her any more — never see her again."

"Yes, sir," she replied, with a brightened look, "I shall see her in heaven."

"But she has gone to heaven already. I trust."

"No, she stops under this tree till they bring me here, and then we are going to heaven together."

It is matter of rejoicing that we are beginning to imitate the example of the Eastern nations in our cemeteries and burial grounds. We have witnessed with grateful satisfaction the change in this respect which has been gradually passing over the public mind and heart within a few years past. Formerly it was the practice to locate the "burying ground" in the most lone, desolate and barren spot that could be found: as if the very space the dead occupied was grudged them. Every thing about it was disagreeable and calculated to repel. What inscriptions and epitaphs on the grave-stones! What emblems — ghastly skulls, cross-bones, and grim skeletons! all eminently fitted to fill the mind, and particularly the young mind, with dismal thoughts, and to make death and the grave subjects most unwelcome, and to be shunned as gloomy and terrifying intruders on the joys of life.

But now all this is passing away; and a better feeling, and a more cheerful faith, are growing up in regard to the dead and the true position and agencies of death — and, as a consequence, the burial place is assuming a more oriental and pleasant aspect; is becoming in the expressive language of the Moravians, "The Valley of Peace." Our Auburns and Greenwoods, our Laurel Hills and Forest Hills, and many other lovely rural spots that have been consecrated as the resting-places of the dead, are cultivating a better taste, and begetting a more Christian feeling. And slowly these beautiful cemeteries with their tall and spreading forest trees, their sweet-smelling shrubbery, their choice flowers that have such a pleasant look, and seem to whisper to the mourning and meditative of comfort and of great hopes; with their significant emblems instinct and eloquent with the truth of immortal purity and blessedness — gradually, but with certain result, out from these, conjoined with a nobler and more cheerful religious faith, there is going an influence corrective of the false and terrifying views of death so long prevalent. And this influence at last will lift up the curtain of clouds from the horizon of the grave, and let in the glorious splendor of life's setting sun upon the shadowy valley, revealing at the other end the golden gates of heaven standing open for the entrance of the liberated and rejoicing soul!

I do not forget, as the preceding pages show, that it is hard to sunder the ties which bind us to the living; and that death has, at the first sight, an unwelcome look, that the grave seen through the mist of tears seems a cold and dark place. But it is for this very reason that I rejoice in the change which has been brought about in the arrangements and appearance of our burial grounds, and which is beginning to make us feel that it is not so sad a thing, after all, to lay the weary body down to rest in so quiet and beautiful a spot, and where Nature folds it to her bosom with so gentle and loving an embrace.

And we are comforted, too, in the thought that the sacred dust of our loved ones rests in so pleasant a place, and that such sweet and hopeful associations and emblems are gathered about it. And we are ready to say,

> "Bring here the dead — a holy spell pervades
> Each grassy dell of these dim solitudes,
> And in these fragrant bowers, and green arcades,
> Religion's deepest, purest influence broods.
> Aye, bring them here, and let the soulless dust
> Rest where there sounds no jar of earthly strife,
> Where all things breathe a gentle, heavenly trust,
> And every bud and leaf with hope is rife,
> And even death itself speaks of Immortal Life!"

www.ingramcontent.com/pod-product-compliance
Lightning Source LLC
Chambersburg PA
CBHW031950230426
43672CB00010B/2118